# THIS BOOK BELONGS TO
## *The Library of*

....................................................................

....................................................................

**Thanks ever so much to each of my cherished readers for investing the time to read this book!**

I know you could have picked from many other books, but you chose this one. So, a big thanks for reading all the way to the end. If you enjoyed this book or received value from it, I'd like to ask you for a favor. Please take a few minutes to **post an honest and heartfelt review on** *Amazon.com.* Your support does make a difference and helps to benefit other people.

*Thanks!*

# Table of Contents

# SUMMARY

Knitting is a textile craft that involves creating fabric by interlocking loops of yarn or thread using knitting needles or a knitting machine. While the exact origins of knitting are still debated among historians, it is believed to have originated in the Middle East or Egypt around the 3rd or 4th century AD. The earliest known examples of knitting have been found in Egypt, where fragments of knitted socks dating back to the 11th century have been discovered.

Knitting gained popularity in Europe during the Middle Ages, particularly in countries like Spain, France, and England. It was initially practiced by men, who were members of knitting guilds and produced knitted garments for the nobility and clergy. However, knitting gradually became a domestic craft, with women taking up the practice and knitting for their families and communities.

Throughout history, knitting has played a significant role in various cultures around the world. In many societies, knitting was not only a practical skill but also a form of artistic expression. Different regions developed their own unique knitting techniques and patterns, which often reflected their cultural heritage and traditions. For example, the Fair Isle knitting technique, characterized by its intricate colorwork patterns, originated in the Fair Isle, a small island in Scotland. Similarly, the Aran knitting style, known for its intricate cable patterns, originated in the Aran Islands off the west coast of Ireland.

Knitting also had social and economic implications. In some communities, knitting was a means of economic survival, providing income for families who relied on selling knitted goods. In times of war or economic hardship, knitting became a way for women to contribute to their households and support their families. During World War I and World War II, knitting played a crucial role in supporting the troops, with women knitting socks, scarves, and other warm garments for soldiers on the front lines.

In addition to its practical and economic significance, knitting has also been associated with various cultural and social movements. In the 19th century, knitting became a symbol of women's empowerment and self-sufficiency. The feminist movement embraced knitting as a way for women to reclaim their domestic skills and challenge traditional gender roles. Knitting circles and groups became spaces for women to gather, share knowledge, and support each other.

Today, knitting continues to be a popular craft practiced by millions of people worldwide. It has evolved beyond its traditional roots and has become a form of self-expression, creativity, and relaxation. Knitting communities and online platforms have emerged, allowing

Knitting is a popular craft that involves creating fabric by interlocking loops of yarn with knitting needles. To successfully knit, you will need a variety of tools and materials.

First and foremost, you will need knitting needles. These come in different sizes and materials, such as metal, wood, or plastic. The size of the needles determines the gauge or tension of your knitting. Thicker needles create larger stitches, while thinner needles create smaller stitches. It is important to choose the right size needles for your project, as it will affect the final size and drape of your knitted fabric.

Next, you will need yarn. Yarn comes in a wide range of colors, textures, and weights. The weight of the yarn refers to its thickness, which can range from super fine to super bulky. The weight of the yarn you choose will depend on the type of project you are working on. For example, a delicate lace shawl may require a fine lace-weight yarn, while a cozy winter sweater may require a bulky yarn.

In addition to knitting needles and yarn, there are several other tools that can be helpful for knitting. One essential tool is a pair of scissors for cutting yarn. You will also need a tapestry needle for weaving in loose ends and sewing pieces of your project together. Stitch markers are useful for marking specific stitches or sections of your knitting, especially when working on complex patterns. A row counter can help you keep track of the number of rows or repeats in your pattern. And if you make a mistake, a crochet hook or knitting needle in a smaller size can be used to fix dropped stitches.

To make your knitting experience more comfortable, you may also want to invest in some additional tools. A knitting bag or project tote can keep all your supplies organized and easily accessible. A knitting gauge or ruler can help you measure your gauge and ensure that your project will turn out the correct size. And if you plan on knitting for long periods of time, ergonomic knitting needles or needle grips can help reduce hand and wrist fatigue.

When it comes to materials, there are endless options for knitters. In addition to traditional wool and acrylic yarns, you can find yarn made from cotton, silk, bamboo, and even recycled materials. Each type of yarn has its own unique properties, such as warmth, softness, or drape, so it is important to choose the right yarn for your project.

In conclusion, knitting requires a variety of tools and materials to create beautiful and functional

Knitting patterns have a rich and fascinating historical perspective that spans centuries. The art of knitting itself dates back to ancient times, with evidence of knitted garments found in archaeological sites from as early as the 11th century. However, it wasn't until the 19th century that knitting patterns as we know them today began to emerge.

In the early days of knitting, patterns were often passed down orally from one generation to the next. Knitting was primarily a practical skill, used to create warm and functional garments for everyday wear. Patterns were simple and repetitive, with basic stitches and techniques being the norm.

As knitting gained popularity and became more of a leisure activity in the 19th century, the demand for more intricate and decorative patterns grew. This led to the development of written knitting patterns, which allowed for more complex designs to be shared and replicated. Knitting pattern books started to appear, providing detailed instructions and charts for creating various stitches and patterns.

During this time, knitting patterns also began to reflect the fashion trends of the era. Knitted lace patterns became particularly popular, as they were seen as a symbol of wealth and status. Knitters would often incorporate intricate lace motifs into their garments, creating delicate and beautiful pieces.

In the early 20th century, knitting patterns became even more accessible with the advent of magazines and catalogs dedicated to knitting. These publications featured a wide range of patterns for different skill levels and styles, catering to the growing community of knitters. Knitting patterns were no longer limited to just garments, but also included accessories such as hats, gloves, and socks.

The mid-20th century saw a shift in knitting patterns, as the focus shifted from intricate designs to more practical and functional pieces. This was influenced by the changing fashion trends and the rise of ready-to-wear clothing. Knitting patterns became simpler and more streamlined, with an emphasis on creating versatile and easy-to-wear garments.

In recent years, knitting patterns have experienced a resurgence in popularity, thanks in part to the rise of online communities and social media. Knitters now have access to a vast array of patterns from all over the world, with designers sharing their creations and techniques online. This has led to a greater diversity in knitting patterns, with styles ranging from traditional to modern and everything in between.

Overall, the historical perspective on knitting patterns showcases the evolution of this craft from a practical skill to a form of artistic expression. From simple and repetitive designs to intricate lace patterns, knitting patterns have

Over the years, knitting patterns have undergone a significant transformation with the advent of technology. The traditional method of creating knitting patterns involved using pen and paper, relying on the knitter's ability to interpret the instructions and visualize the final product. However, with the introduction of technology, knitting patterns have become more accessible, precise, and customizable.

One of the most notable advancements in knitting patterns is the availability of digital platforms and software specifically designed for creating and sharing patterns. Knitters can now find a plethora of websites, apps, and software that offer a wide range of patterns, from simple designs to intricate lacework. These platforms not only provide a vast library of patterns but also allow users to customize and modify existing patterns to suit their preferences.

The integration of technology into knitting patterns has also made it easier for knitters to follow instructions accurately. Digital patterns often include interactive features such as hyperlinks, videos, and images that provide step-by-step guidance. This eliminates the need for guesswork and ensures that even novice knitters can successfully complete complex patterns. Additionally, digital patterns can be easily zoomed in or out, making it easier for individuals with visual impairments to follow along.

Another significant development in knitting patterns is the emergence of charting software. Traditionally, complex stitch patterns were represented using written instructions, which could be confusing and time-consuming to decipher. However, charting software allows knitters to visualize the pattern through graphical representations, making it much simpler to understand and execute intricate designs. This technology has revolutionized the way knitters approach complex patterns, enabling them to create stunning and intricate garments with ease.

Furthermore, technology has facilitated the sharing and collaboration of knitting patterns among the knitting community. Online platforms and social media groups have become hubs for knitters to connect, share their creations, and exchange patterns. This has created a vibrant and supportive community where knitters can learn from each other, seek inspiration, and collaborate on projects. The ability to share patterns digitally has also eliminated the need for physical copies, reducing paper waste and contributing to a more sustainable knitting practice.

In conclusion, technology has had a profound impact on the evolution of knitting patterns. From the accessibility and customization offered by digital platforms to the precision and clarity provided by charting software, technology has made knitting patterns more user-friendly and versatile. Additionally, the ability to share patterns online has fostered a sense of community and collaboration among knitters worldwide. As technology continues to advance, it is exciting to envision how knitting patterns will further evolve

Knitting abbreviations and symbols are essential for understanding and following knitting patterns. They provide a shorthand way of conveying instructions and techniques, making it easier for knitters to read and interpret patterns accurately.

Abbreviations are commonly used in knitting patterns to represent specific stitches or techniques. For example, k is the abbreviation for knit stitch, p is the abbreviation for purl stitch, and yo is the abbreviation for yarn over. These abbreviations are used throughout patterns to indicate which stitches to work and in what order.

Symbols, on the other hand, are visual representations of stitches or techniques. They are often used in charts or diagrams to provide a clear and concise visual guide for knitters. Symbols can represent different types of stitches, such as knit, purl, yarn over, decrease, or increase stitches. They can also indicate specific techniques, such as cables, lace patterns, or colorwork.

Understanding knitting abbreviations and symbols is crucial for successfully following knitting patterns. Without this knowledge, patterns can be confusing and difficult to decipher. By familiarizing yourself with common knitting abbreviations and symbols, you can easily read and interpret patterns, ensuring that your knitting projects turn out as intended.

To learn knitting abbreviations and symbols, it is helpful to refer to a knitting glossary or guidebook. These resources provide explanations and illustrations of various abbreviations and symbols, making it easier to understand their meanings and how to execute them in your knitting.

Additionally, practicing with simple patterns that incorporate different abbreviations and symbols can help reinforce your understanding. By working through these patterns, you can become more comfortable with the terminology and techniques, gradually building your knitting skills and confidence.

In conclusion, knitting abbreviations and symbols are essential tools for knitters. They allow for clear and concise communication of instructions and techniques in knitting patterns. By familiarizing yourself with these abbreviations and symbols, you can confidently read and interpret patterns, enabling you to create beautiful and intricate knitted projects.

The exploration of geometric shapes and symmetry in knitting is a fascinating and creative endeavor that allows knitters to push the boundaries of traditional knitting techniques and create visually stunning and intricate designs. By incorporating geometric shapes and symmetry into their knitting projects, knitters can create unique and eye-catching patterns that showcase their artistic skills and attention to detail.

One of the key aspects of exploring geometric shapes in knitting is understanding the different types of shapes that can be created using various knitting techniques. From simple shapes like squares and triangles to more complex shapes like hexagons and octagons, knitters can experiment with different stitch patterns and color combinations to create geometric designs that are both visually appealing and structurally sound.

Symmetry, on the other hand, adds an additional layer of complexity and sophistication to knitted designs. By incorporating symmetrical elements into their knitting projects, knitters can create patterns that are balanced and harmonious. This can be achieved through the use of mirrored stitch patterns, where the same sequence of stitches is repeated on both sides of the fabric, or through the use of symmetrical color placements, where colors are arranged in a symmetrical manner.

The exploration of geometric shapes and symmetry in knitting also opens up a world of possibilities for creating three-dimensional objects. By combining different shapes and utilizing techniques such as short rows and increases/decreases, knitters can create knitted sculptures and objects that defy traditional notions of what can be achieved with yarn and needles. From geometric-inspired hats and shawls to intricate knitted toys and home decor items, the possibilities are truly endless.

Furthermore, the exploration of geometric shapes and symmetry in knitting can also be a means of self-expression and personal storytelling. Knitters can use these design elements to convey a specific message or to reflect their own unique style and personality. Whether it's incorporating a favorite geometric pattern into a sweater or using symmetrical color placements to represent a personal journey, knitting becomes a powerful medium for artistic expression.

In conclusion, the exploration of geometric shapes and symmetry in knitting offers knitters a world of creative possibilities. From creating visually stunning patterns to pushing the boundaries of traditional knitting techniques, knitters can use these design elements to create unique and captivating projects. Whether it's through the use of different shapes, symmetrical elements, or three-dimensional designs, the exploration of geometric shapes and symmetry in knitting allows knitters to showcase their artistic skills and create truly one-of-a-kind pieces.

Color theory is a fundamental concept in the world of art and design, and it also plays a significant role in the realm of knitting. Understanding the basics of color theory can greatly enhance your knitting projects, allowing you to create visually appealing and harmonious color combinations.

At its core, color theory is the study of how colors interact with each other and how they can be combined to create different visual effects. It involves understanding the color wheel, color relationships, and the psychological impact of different colors. By applying these principles to your knitting, you can create stunning and well-balanced color schemes.

The color wheel is a useful tool in color theory, and it consists of twelve colors arranged in a circular format. The primary colors, which are red, blue, and yellow, are located at equal distances from each other on the wheel. These colors cannot be created by mixing other colors together. Secondary colors, such as orange, green, and purple, are created by mixing two primary colors together. Tertiary colors, such as red-orange, yellow-green, and blue-violet, are created by mixing a primary color with a secondary color.

Understanding color relationships is crucial when it comes to selecting colors for your knitting projects. There are several types of color relationships, including complementary, analogous, and monochromatic. Complementary colors are located directly opposite each other on the color wheel, such as red and green or blue and orange. When used together, complementary colors create a high contrast and vibrant effect. Analogous colors, on the other hand, are located next to each other on the color wheel, such as blue and green or red and orange. These colors create a harmonious and cohesive look when used together. Monochromatic color schemes involve using different shades and tints of a single color, creating a subtle and sophisticated effect.

In addition to understanding the color wheel and color relationships, it is also important to consider the psychological impact of different colors. Colors can evoke certain emotions and moods, and this can greatly influence the overall feel of your knitting project. For example, warm colors like red and orange are often associated with energy and excitement, while cool colors like blue and green are associated with calmness and tranquility. By carefully selecting colors that align with the desired mood or theme of your knitting project, you can create a more impactful and meaningful piece.

When applying color theory to knitting, there are several ways to incorporate different colors into your projects. You can choose to use multiple colors in a single

When it comes to knitting, there is a wide range of techniques and patterns that can be used to create different textures in your projects. One of the most popular ways to add texture to your knitting is through the use of cables. Cables are created by crossing stitches over each other, creating a twisted effect that adds depth and interest to your knitting. They can be simple or complex, depending on the pattern you choose, and can be used to create a variety of designs, from simple braids to intricate Celtic knots.

Another way to add texture to your knitting is through the use of lace. Lace patterns are created by intentionally creating holes in your knitting, which can be achieved through a variety of techniques, such as yarn overs and decreases. Lace patterns can range from delicate and intricate to bold and geometric, and can be used to create a variety of effects, from airy and lightweight shawls to intricate and detailed garments.

In addition to cables and lace, there are many other techniques and patterns that can be used to add texture to your knitting. For example, you can use different stitch patterns, such as seed stitch or moss stitch, to create a bumpy or textured effect. You can also experiment with different yarns and fibers, as certain yarns can create more texture than others. For example, a yarn with a high twist or a boucle yarn can create a more textured fabric.

When exploring different textures in knitting, it's important to consider the overall effect you want to achieve and the purpose of your project. For example, if you're knitting a cozy sweater, you may want to use cables or textured stitch patterns to add warmth and interest. On the other hand, if you're knitting a delicate lace shawl, you may want to focus on creating a lightweight and airy fabric.

Overall, exploring different textures in knitting allows you to unleash your creativity and add depth and interest to your projects. Whether you choose to experiment with cables, lace, or other techniques, the possibilities are endless. So grab your needles and yarn, and start exploring the world of texture in knitting!

Knitting, a centuries-old craft, has gained popularity not only for its ability to create beautiful and functional items but also for its therapeutic benefits. Many individuals have discovered that knitting can serve as a form of meditation and stress relief, offering a respite from the demands and pressures of daily life.

Engaging in knitting requires focus and concentration, as one must carefully manipulate the yarn and needles to create intricate patterns and stitches. This level of concentration helps to divert attention away from stressful thoughts and worries, allowing the mind to enter a state of calm and relaxation. The repetitive nature of knitting also contributes to its meditative qualities, as the rhythmic movements of the hands and the soothing click of the needles create a sense of flow and mindfulness.

Furthermore, the tactile nature of knitting provides a sensory experience that can be incredibly soothing. The softness of the yarn, the gentle pull of the needles, and the satisfaction of seeing a project take shape all contribute to a sense of comfort and tranquility. The act of knitting can be likened to a form of self-care, as it allows individuals to engage in a creative and productive activity that brings them joy and a sense of accomplishment.

In addition to its meditative qualities, knitting has been shown to have numerous physical and mental health benefits. Research has indicated that knitting can help reduce stress levels, lower blood pressure, and alleviate symptoms of anxiety and depression. The repetitive motions involved in knitting stimulate the release of endorphins, which are natural mood-boosting chemicals in the brain. This can lead to an overall improvement in mental well-being and a greater sense of calm and contentment.

Moreover, knitting has been found to enhance cognitive function and improve focus and attention. The complex patterns and techniques involved in knitting require mental agility and problem-solving skills, which can help sharpen the mind and improve memory. This makes knitting not only a relaxing activity but also a mentally stimulating one, providing a holistic approach to self-care and stress management.

In a world that is increasingly fast-paced and digitally-driven, knitting offers a much-needed respite from the constant stimulation and demands of modern life. It provides individuals with an opportunity to slow down, disconnect from technology, and engage in a mindful and creative activity. Whether it's knitting a cozy scarf, a warm blanket, or a delicate sweater, the process of knitting can be a deeply rewarding and therapeutic experience.

In conclusion, knitting as a form of meditation and stress relief offers a multitude of benefits for both the mind and body.

 Online and offline knitting communities play a significant role in fostering a sense of belonging, creativity, and skill development among knitting enthusiasts. These communities provide a platform for individuals to connect, share their passion for knitting, and learn from one another.

Online knitting communities have gained immense popularity in recent years due to the convenience and accessibility they offer. These communities typically exist on social media platforms, dedicated knitting forums, and websites. They provide a space for knitters from all around the world to come together, regardless of their geographical location or time zone. This global reach allows for a diverse range of perspectives, techniques, and patterns to be shared, enriching the overall knitting experience.

Within online knitting communities, members can engage in discussions, seek advice, and share their completed projects. This virtual interaction fosters a sense of camaraderie and support among knitters, as they can connect with like-minded individuals who understand their passion and challenges. Additionally, online communities often organize virtual knitting circles or live-streamed tutorials, allowing members to participate in real-time knitting sessions and learn new skills from experienced knitters.

Offline knitting communities, on the other hand, provide a more traditional and intimate setting for knitters to connect. These communities often take the form of local knitting groups, knitting clubs, or workshops held in physical spaces such as yarn stores or community centers. Offline communities offer the opportunity for face-to-face interactions, allowing knitters to form deeper connections and friendships.

In offline knitting communities, members can gather regularly to knit together, share patterns, and exchange tips and tricks. These gatherings create a supportive and encouraging environment where knitters can learn from one another, troubleshoot challenges, and celebrate their accomplishments. Offline communities also provide a space for knitters to showcase their work through local exhibitions or craft fairs, further fostering a sense of pride and accomplishment.

Both online and offline knitting communities contribute to the growth and development of knitting skills. Through the sharing of patterns, techniques, and experiences, knitters can expand their knowledge and improve their craft. These communities also serve as a source of inspiration, as members can explore different knitting styles, experiment with new patterns, and challenge themselves to try new techniques.

In conclusion, online and offline knitting communities offer invaluable support, inspiration, and learning opportunities for knitting enthusiasts. Whether through virtual interactions or face-to-face gatherings, these communities foster a sense of belonging and provide a platform for knitters to connect, share, and grow together.

# Chapter 1

I checked my watch for the tenth time and said, "They'll be here any second. I'm so excited! Are you excited? I am." I clasped my hands together and looked at my sister, Erin.

She gave me a sideways look. "I'm not as excited as you. What's wrong with you tonight? You keep grinning to yourself and jigging from side to side. Have you been drinking?" She moved closer and sniffed me.

"No, I haven't been drinking." I glanced around the café which we co-owned. It was currently undergoing an extensive renovation. I continued, "But look at everything. The café is nearly finished. The tables and chairs are all here. And we're going to have our first-ever craft evening in our new café! I could burst with joy."

Erin shook her head at me. "Your voice is going all screechy. Calm down. Look at me; I'm the picture of serenity." She pointed at her face and gave me a serene smile.

I put my hand on my stomach and grinned some more. "I've got butterflies. They're dancing like crazy in my stomach."

Erin's eyes narrowed. "Hang on a minute. You've only become this excited in the last ten minutes. Has your giddy condition got something to do with your psychic abilities? Are your psychic senses tingling and having a funny effect on you? Is it something to do with our café? "

I frowned and looked around us. "I'm not sure. Now that you've said that, I can honestly say I'm not feeling giddy about the café or the work that's been done on it. It's been a bit of a pain to get everything finished."

"It still isn't finished. According to my ever-helpful husband, it'll be another week before we can open the café to customers. Karis, are you excited about the kitchen? I love it, but does the thought of those shiny new appliances get you hot under the collar?" She smiled. "This is a weird conversation."

I looked over to where the kitchen was. It had everything Erin needed to make those delicious cakes of hers. I said, "I'm not getting even a flicker of joy as I think about the kitchen. Sorry."

"What about the seating area with those new sofas and tables over in our relaxing area? Is that area making your temperature rise?"

"It is a lovely part of the café, but no, it's not doing a thing for me." I studied the elderly woman who was near the sofas. Peggy Marshall was in charge of tonight's craft event and she was making sure everything was ready for our clients. I thought about the event which would start soon, grinned and then turned to face Erin.

Erin was one step ahead of me and said, "You're thinking about tonight's event, aren't you? Something about Peggy's knitting class is getting you all hot and bothered."

"I wouldn't use those words. But you are right. There's something about this evening which is affecting me. I'm getting more excited by the minute. I can't control it."

Erin nodded. "You'll be getting one of your visions soon. I'm sure of it." She folded her arms and gave me a stern look. "I hope you don't have another one of your murder visions. I don't want a violent act occurring in our café. Karis, if someone's about to be murdered, can you make sure it happens outside? I don't want any blood on the new furnishings."

I shook my head at her. "I can't control my visions, certainly not the murder ones." I grimaced. "If there is going to be a murder, I hope it doesn't involve knitting needles. We've got a lot of those on the tables."

"Maybe we should move them," Erin suggested. "You should have a good look at the people who are coming here tonight. When they come through the door, have a thorough stare at them. Watch out for any suspicious-looking people. See if any of them smell weird."

"Potential murderers don't smell any different to normal people."

Erin gave me a wise look. "How do you know? Have you studied them? Have you smelled them all?"

"Who's talking about murderers?" Peggy said as she came over to us. She sighed heavily. "Karis, you haven't had one of your visions, have you? Is someone going to get bumped off tonight during my knitting class? Do you know what time it's going to happen?"

"I haven't had a vision," I began. "I'm just—"

Peggy interrupted me, "I hope it's at the end of my class. I've got a detailed schedule of what I'm going to do. Will the murder weapon be a knitting needle? Will it be a metal one or a wooden one? I've got both kinds on the tables. Blood can be wiped off a metal one, but it'll stain a wooden one. Where's the murder going to happen? I hope the sofas don't get damaged. They're brand new."

I put my hand on her arm to halt the flow of words. "Peggy, I haven't had a vision. I've been experiencing a high level of excitement, that's all. I'm excited about the evening, and I know it's going to go well. You've got everything under control."

Peggy's brow furrowed. "Are you sure you haven't had a murder vision?"

"A murder vision? Tonight?" Robbie, Erin's husband, appeared behind us. "I hope no one gets blood on my new walls. It took me forever to paint these walls, and those were the last pots they had at the DIY place. If those walls get ruined, I'll have to paint the whole café again."

All feelings of excitement had left me now. I was full of irritation instead. I proclaimed, "I haven't had a vision of someone being murdered! Okay? Have you all got that?"

Peggy rubbed her ear. "There's no need to shout." She turned to face Robbie. "Have you got the recording equipment ready? Is it all set to record the class? Did you look at my schedule? Have you memorised it? I'll be standing near the sofas, to begin with. I'll be sitting at other times, and then walking about. You need to keep up with me. The readers of my blog are waiting with bated breath for the video of this evening's event. I don't want you making a pig's ear of it, Robbie Terris."

Robbie gave her a broad smile. "I won't. I have memorised your schedule. I have triple checked my equipment. I've been practising my recording skills on my wife." He winked at Erin.

She blushed and looked away.

Peggy tapped Robbie roughly on the arm. "I hope you haven't been making any rude videos. I don't want you putting the wrong one on my blog by mistake. I'm not running that kind of internet business."

"There's no need to worry," Robbie advised. "There's been no funny business going on with Erin and me. I just wanted to capture her radiant beauty as she progresses through her pregnancy." His gaze softened as he looked at Erin. "I didn't think you could get any more beautiful, my love. But each day, you're becoming more breathtaking."

Erin blushed some more. "Stop it, you fool."

Peggy rapped Robbie on the arm again. "Get your attention off your wife and on to me. My readers are expecting great things from me. You need to capture my every move."

Robbie chuckled. "Being an internet sensation has gone to your head, Peggy Marshall. What time are your clients getting here?"

"Seven o'clock," Peggy replied. "We've got five minutes. I've got everything prepared. Erin, have you got the refreshments ready?"

"I have," Erin replied.

Peggy looked at Robbie. "Is your recording equipment fully charged?"

"It is," Robbie replied with an increasing smile. "I won't let you down."

"You'd better not," Peggy replied darkly. "Karis, you know what you're doing, don't you? Some of my clients are total beginners. They'll need a lot of help."

"I know what is expected of me," I replied.

"Good, good. Then we're ready to go." Peggy patted her hair. "Do I look okay? Do I look camera-ready?"

We all nodded at Peggy.

The door to the café opened.

Peggy gasped. "They're here! Action stations, everyone." She gave me a stern look. "Karis, don't let anyone get murdered tonight."

"I'll try my best."

Peggy rushed over to the café door with a huge smile of welcome on her face. Robbie and Erin were right behind her.

And that's when I got a psychic vision.

# Chapter 2

My surroundings faded.

I was sitting on a sofa in a warm room. Something was on my lap. My stomach leapt with excitement as I looked at it.

It was a knitting pattern.

I felt immense relief at having it in my possession. I'd been waiting ages for it to arrive.

I picked it up and studied it. The pattern was for a stylish twin set. The model was wearing the jumper and cardigan with elegance. A string of pearls adorned her neck. She was staring happily at something in the distance.

My attention went to the wool at my side. It was light blue. I picked a ball up and placed it next to my cheek. It was soft. I smiled. How would he feel when he saw me in this colour? Would he say I looked like a Hollywood star? I hoped he would.

Warm feelings of joy and happiness rushed through me. He was going to love seeing me in this twin set. He'd say I looked just like—

My thoughts abruptly stopped as I felt a sharp nudge at my side. I jumped when I saw Erin glowering at me.

Erin hissed, "Karis, what are you doing? Why are you stroking your cheek like that? Did you have a vision?"

I nodded and quickly looked around the café. "I'll have to tell you about it later. Peggy is giving me a dark look. I'd better go over to her."

Erin grabbed my arm and whispered, "Was it about a murder? Is there going to be one tonight? Tell me."

"It wasn't about a murder. It was about a knitting pattern." I smiled at the memory and how eager I'd felt about that pattern.

"A knitting pattern?" Erin's eyebrows rose. "You've been going all soppy over a knitting pattern? You need to get out more."

Before I could defend myself or explain the vision more, Erin walked away and headed for the kitchen.

I went over to Peggy who was standing near the sofas. The people who had entered a few minutes ago were sitting on the sofas. They were taking their coats off while keeping their wide-eyed looks on Peggy. They were looking at her as if she was a superstar. I suppose she was to them. She'd become quite a celebrity with her blog. Peggy had lived next to Mum for years. Erin and I had grown up with her in our lives. She was like a second mum to us.

Peggy saw me approaching and announced, "This is Karis Booth. She co-owns this business with her sister, Erin. I told you about Karis on my blog."

Some of the seated people gave me knowing looks and I wondered what Peggy had written about me. She wrote her blog posts every day, but I didn't always have time to read them.

"Hello," I said to them.

Peggy continued, "Karis will be on hand to help anyone if they need it. She's an accomplished knitter."

"Thanks to you," I said. I addressed the seated clients. "Peggy taught me to knit when I was young. She's an excellent teacher. She's very patient and explains everything clearly."

An older man nodded to himself and gave Peggy an admiring look.

"That's enough about me," Peggy said. A pink tinge came to her cheeks. "Let's get on. We'll start with the basic stitch for those who are new to knitting. I hope you more experienced knitters will be patient with me while I do that. I've got a wide variety of knitting patterns and wool if any of you want to make a start on your own projects. They're laid out on the tables over there. Help yourselves."

At the mention of the knitting patterns, my heart missed a beat. I had to find that pattern for the twin set. I looked at the patterns which were arranged on the nearby tables. Urgency rushed through me. I had to look at those patterns right now. I made a move forwards.

I felt a hand on my arm. Peggy said quietly, "Where are you going? I need help with the beginners."

I didn't know at this stage whether my vision was important, so I decided not to tell Peggy about it yet. It could wait. I said, "Where do you want me?"

"Follow me."

Robbie appeared on the scene. He had a smudge of chocolate around his lips. He said to Peggy, "I'm here. Ready to record."

Peggy's eyes narrowed. "Robbie, have you been eating cake that's supposed to be for my clients? No, don't answer that. I already know the answer. Come with me. I'm going to start with the beginners. Get your recording equipment ready."

Robbie shot a grin at me. "I'm always in trouble with Peggy. I'll have to be on my best behaviour."

"Me too," I added.

Some of the clients were now standing by the table of patterns and looking through them. My palms suddenly felt itchy. I wanted to be over there with them. I wanted to be looking through those patterns. What if someone found my pattern before I did? I couldn't have that.

Peggy's loud voice brought my attention back to her. "Karis, come over here and let me introduce you to everyone. This is Tom. He's a beginner." She smiled at the older man who'd been nodding at my words earlier. Peggy said to him, "Thank you for all your comments on my blog, Tom. You are too kind."

Tom gave her a huge smile which was almost manic. He gushed, "I meant every word. Your blog inspires me every day. I read each entry more than once. Just like you, I want to fulfil my creative side. It's been lying dormant inside me for years. You've woken it up, Peggy. I can feel my creative juices flowing as we speak."

"That's nice," Peggy said politely. "Karis, you sit next to Tom. Show him the basic knitting stitch." She swiftly moved away. I heard a small chuckle coming from Robbie as he filmed the exchange.

I took a seat next to Tom. It was obvious he didn't want me to be the one teaching him. Despite his indifference to me, I remained patient and polite as I taught him the basic stitches using a pair of large needles and chunky wool.

Tom barely paid me any attention. His eyes were on Peggy as she chatted to other people. He asked me various questions about Peggy, such as how long I'd known her, and what her favourite TV programmes were. I answered swiftly and tried to get Tom's attention back on his work. I stopped answering his questions completely when he asked if Peggy was single.

I gave Tom a stern look. "This isn't a dating evening. You're here to learn how to knit. Am I wasting my time? Do you want to learn or not?"

Peggy picked that moment to return. "Karis, please don't talk to Tom like that. You're scaring him." She gave him a kind smile. "Would you like me to take over from Karis?"

Tom's face lit up with joy. "Yes! I would! Yes!"

I quickly stood up and handed the knitting needles to Peggy before she changed her mind. I was in her bad books for sure now, but I didn't care. I had to find that pattern.

I headed towards the table. I didn't get very far.

Erin came towards me with two plates piled high with sandwiches. "Karis, give me a hand with these. I think I've made too much, as always." She shoved the plates at me.

I didn't have a choice as to whether I wanted to hold them or not. I took them and said, "But I wanted to look at the knitting patterns."

"Not the knitting pattern talk again! Put those plates on that table over there. Then come into the kitchen and get the cakes. Once those are out, you can get on with the tea and coffee."

I gave her a scowl. "Stop being so bossy."

She rested a hand on her stomach. "I'm taking it easy. That's what you've been telling me for weeks. You know full well I've got twins in here. I need to rest as much as possible."

I sighed. "I know. Sorry. I don't know what's wrong with me."

Erin was looking at the clients around the café and counting silently. "Didn't Peggy say there would be twelve here tonight? I can only see eleven."

"She did say twelve. Perhaps someone is running late. I'll take this over to the table now and get those cakes in a minute."

Erin nodded and walked back to the kitchen.

I placed the plates on a table which was a short distance from the knitting area. Peggy had insisted on food being away from her supplies. She said she didn't want crumbs and half-eaten sandwiches mixed amongst her precious wool.

I turned towards the kitchen but stopped moving when the café door opened. A young woman dressed in black came hurrying in. Her long hair was black and she had a variety of facial piercings. Plastic bags dangled from her hands.

Peggy stood up and called out to her, "Jade! There you are. I thought you weren't going to make it. Come over here. Let me introduce you to everyone."

Jade gave Peggy a bashful smile and moved closer. "Hello, Peggy. I'm sorry I'm late. I missed my bus."

"Don't worry about being late; you're here now. Come here. Let me get a good look at you," Peggy said. "Isn't it lovely to finally meet in the flesh? I feel as if I've known you and everyone else for years."

Tom piped up, "I feel like I've been waiting for you all my life, Peggy."

Peggy ignored Tom and said to Jade, "What have you got in those bags? Is it your food shopping? Do you need to put anything in the fridge? You can use the café ones."

Jade lifted the bags higher. "These are knitting patterns. Really old ones. I've been looking in charity shops recently. That's where I get most of my clothes from. When I saw these patterns, I thought you might like them."

Using Erin's previous expression, my psychic senses began to tingle. I moved towards Jade, took the bags from her and announced, "I'll look after these. Help yourself to food." I moved away from the curious stares that came my way and hurried towards the far side of the room.

I could barely contain my excitement as I knelt on the carpet and carefully tipped the contents out. Many knitting patterns slithered to the floor. Some were quite tatty-looking. Many had stains on them. I did wonder for a second if I should be wearing rubber gloves.

I pushed the patterns around the carpet to separate them. My heart was beating ten to the dozen as I scoured the images.

There! There it was! My pattern! The very one I'd seen in my vision.

I picked it up, held it to my chest and jumped to my feet. I cried out in joy and spun around on the spot.

There was a sudden silence. I stopped spinning and saw that everyone was staring at me.

I didn't care. This pattern was important to me. Really important. I could sense it deep down in my bones. Without any shred of doubt, I knew that whoever had owned this pattern desperately needed my help.

What that help was – I didn't know.

Who needed my help? Again, I didn't know.

But I would work it out. Somehow.

# Chapter 3

The rest of the evening seemed to drag at an impossibly slow rate. As pleased as I was that we had customers for our craft evening, I was impatient for the event to end so I could go home and make a start on the knitting pattern.

Eagle-eyed Peggy noticed my agitation and took me to one side during a refreshment break.

She said to me, "What's got into you? You keep looking at the door as if you want to make a break for it. Have you got somewhere important to go?" Her glance went to the knitting pattern which I was holding to my chest. "Has it got something to do with that pattern which you're guarding with your life? Come on; spit it out. I know something is going on."

"I'm not sure it means anything," I began. I told her about my vision concerning the pattern. Peggy had always been supportive when it came to my visions.

When I'd finished telling her, she said, "I see. This pattern must be important for some reason. Let me look at it."

I handed it over.

Peggy examined it. "A twin set. You don't see many of these about nowadays. They were all the rage years ago. This pattern isn't too complicated. There's a bit of cable work, but you can manage that. Come over to my stash of wool and let's see if we can find you the right colour. You can make a start on this straight away." She gave me the pattern back.

"But I'm supposed to be helping you," I protested.

Peggy gave me a look. "No offence, but you haven't been much use to me since you found that pattern." She looked over her shoulder at the knitting group. "They're doing really well. I can manage on my own with them." She looked back at me. "You need to get on with this pattern as soon as possible. With it being a jumper and a cardigan, it's going to take you a while to get through it. Come on. Let's find you some wool."

I knew I should have argued with her and insisted on helping her with her knitting group, but there was a part of me which knew I had to complete the twin set quickly. Or at least make a start on it.

I followed Peggy over to the storage area and she pulled out the bottom drawer. Balls of wool were lined up neatly inside. I couldn't see the shade of blue that I needed, so Peggy opened the next drawer.

She said, "I've got some more wool at home too. I've been collecting it for weeks. Have a good rummage about in this drawer. I think there's some blue wool at the back."

I began to move balls of wool out of the way. My palm felt itchy as I did so. I was getting closer to something.

"That's it!" I declared. "That's the exact shade I need!"

Peggy gave me a concerned look. "Okay. Keep your voice down. How many do you need?"

I checked the pattern and then gave Peggy the number.

She counted the balls of wool in front of her. Her eyebrows rose. "That's the exact number that's here. Talk about a coincidence. Let me pop these into a bag for you." She handed a ball to me. "Take this one now. Get yourself a pair of knitting needles and find somewhere quiet to sit. And stop grinning to yourself like that. You look as if you're a sandwich short of a picnic."

I took the wool and went over to the table where the knitting needles were. I was aware of people from the knitting group giving me concerned looks, but that didn't bother me. I was used to it. I'd been having psychic visions all my life and I was often on the receiving end of many concerned looks.

I went over to an armchair at the side of the room and settled down into it. Robbie came over with a cup in his hand. He placed it on the table at my side. He said quietly, "Erin's told me about your latest premonition. Here's a cup of tea to keep you going. Do you want anything to eat? Erin's made a feast of treats."

"No, thanks." My attention was already on the pattern.

I felt Robbie looking at it too. He chuckled. "My gran used to knit things like that. She even had a set of pearls to go with her creations. Not real pearls, of course. Rightio, I'll leave you to it. Let me know if you need anything."

I shot him a swift smile. "Thanks, Robbie."

As soon as he'd walked away, I examined the pattern more closely. One of the sizes on the pattern had been ringed in pencil. The circle around the number didn't quite close. The same pencilled ring had been used throughout the pattern to indicate which size to use. Whoever had used this pattern was the same size as me. That was useful.

As I began casting on, the butterflies in my stomach did a happy dance again. The earlier feelings of excitement returned to me and an image of a smiling young man flittered into my mind. As soon as I concentrated on his face, the image faded.

I soon had the ribbed hem completed. My fingers felt light and energetic as I continued to knit. It was almost like the knitting needles were becoming part of me. Calmness and certainty descended on me as I completed row after row. I'd forgotten how relaxing it was to knit.

I'd almost completed the back segment of the jumper when I felt a tap on my shoulder. Peggy smiled down at me. "Karis, how are you doing?"

I lifted up the knitted piece for her inspection.

She smiled. "You've done a great job on that. Do you want to take it home with you? We're closing up now."

I blinked at her in surprise. "But the evening's only just started."

She waved her hand at the empty sofas. "It ended thirty minutes ago. Everyone's gone home."

"Have they? I didn't hear them."

"I'm not surprised. You've been in a trance for the last few hours. You've been quite a good advert for me."

"An advert? What do you mean?" I began to knit the next row.

"I was telling my group about how relaxing knitting was, and how it calms your mind. I pointed to you to prove my point. For the last few hours, you've had a peaceful look on your face as you completed line after line. It was like you were meditating or something. I didn't want to interrupt you now, but I have to get home. Erin and Robbie do too. They're in the kitchen."

"Are they cleaning up? Let me finish this row and I'll give them a hand. I can't believe I've been sitting here for hours and not helping anyone."

Peggy rested a hand on my shoulder. "You've got this work to do. Erin and Robbie know that, and so do I. I can get a taxi home if you want to stay here a bit longer. I've packed that wool up for you."

I finished the row and stuck the needles into the ball of wool. I said, "You're not getting a taxi. I'll drive you. You can tell me all about the evening on the way back. From what I saw, it was a great success." I paused. "I think you've got a secret admirer in Tom."

Peggy let out a small laugh. "He can admire me all he wants, but my Jeff is still in my heart. And he will be until the day I die and join him wherever he might be. I know he's waiting for me somewhere."

Erin and Robbie came out of the kitchen and headed towards us.

Robbie said, "Come on, Karis, clear off home and take this old lady with you. Erin and I want to go home and cuddle up together. It's taken all my willpower to keep my hands off her tonight. Look how beautiful she is."

Erin gave him a gentle push. "You are a ninny." She looked over at me. "Have you had any more visions yet? Any scenes of murder popped into your head? Any deceased bodies you want to tell us about?"

I shook my head. "Nothing like that, thank goodness. I'm sorry I haven't helped you much tonight."

Erin put her arm around Robbie's waist. "We've managed just fine. Off you go before I throw you out. I need some alone time with my wonderful husband."

I gathered my things together and then helped Peggy into the car with her belongings. It took several trips. At one point, I noticed her carrying bottles of gin and boxes of chocolate. I asked her where they'd come from.

A pink tinge came to her cheeks as she answered, "It's those lovely people in my knitting group. They've already paid a fee for the night; they didn't have to give me gifts too. But they insisted on it. They've been too kind. You'll have to share these chocolates with me. I won't be able to manage them all on my own. I'll be able to manage the gin, though."

As we drove home, Peggy told me how the class went. Everyone enjoyed it, and they promised to send her photos of their finished products.

Peggy said, "Robbie has already uploaded a video to our website, and there have been many comments. I'm going to read them when I get home." Her voice softened. "I never thought my life could change so much, and especially at my age. I'm so busy all the time. And I love it. It's all thanks to you. I'm glad you got a divorce and used your settlement money on the café. Perhaps that ex-husband of yours was actually useful in a roundabout sort of way." She gave a sniff of disapproval. "I must be tired if I'm thinking kindly about Gavin Booth. As soon as I've read those comments online, I'll be taking to my bed. I suggest you do the same. Don't stay up all night knitting."

"I won't," I replied.

We stopped outside the semi-detached houses where we lived. Mum owned the one on the left, and Peggy owned the one on the right. Mum was in a care home now and hadn't lived here for two years. Since getting divorced, I'd moved back to the family home. I loved being back here.

Despite Peggy's protests, I walked her to the door and waited until she was inside. She handed me a couple of boxes of chocolate before she said goodnight and closed the door. I collected my belongings from the car, made my way to Mum's house and let myself in.

I'd told Peggy I wouldn't stay up all night knitting, but I knew I would stay up at least half the night with my craftwork. I had to get this twin set completed. There was an urgency to it.

Erin had insisted that I bring some cake home. Once I'd put that in the fridge, I made myself a cup of coffee. Then I settled down in the living room with my knitting project.

I'd been knitting for a few hours when a soft knock sounded on the front door. I froze. Who was calling at this time of the night? If it was a burglar, it was a polite one.

Holding on to the only weapon I had, I moved cautiously towards the front door. I made sure the safety chain was on, and then I slowly opened it.

# Chapter 4

DCI Sebastian Parker was standing on the doorstep. In a calm voice, he said, "Lower your weapon, Mrs Booth." He frowned. "Is that a knitting needle?"

I put the knitting needle behind my back and opened the door wider.

Seb Parker had been my childhood friend, but that had changed when we went to high school. I'd never shied away from my psychic abilities at high school, and that had been a mistake. My peers had made fun of me, even Seb. He bitterly regretted his behaviour now. I knew his remorse was sincere and we were back to being friends.

"Come in," I said to him. "What are you doing here at this time?"

He stepped into the house. "I've been working a late shift at the station. There's a mountain of paperwork to get through. I don't even think I've made a dent in it yet. I was on my way home when I saw your light on. Is everything okay? Why are you up so late?"

I quickly told him about my vision and the knitting pattern. I concluded, "I can't rest until I finish the twin set." I tucked the knitting needle under my arm and flexed my aching fingers. "I can keep going for a few more hours."

Seb said, "Would you like some company? I'm not tired enough to sleep yet."

I gave him a smile. "I would love some company, thanks. Would you put the kettle on, please? If you're hungry, there's some cake in the fridge. Erin made it for tonight's craft event."

"Oh, I forgot about that event. How did it go? I've been reading Peggy's blog. She's got many followers."

I moved over to the sofa and picked my knitting back up. "I'll tell you about it when you bring the tea in."

He laughed. "I get the hint. Won't be long." He headed towards the kitchen.

I'd completed three more rows by the time he returned. My fingers were aching a bit more now. When Seb handed me a cup, I wrapped my hands around it in the hope of giving my hands some reviving heat treatment.

Seb sat in the armchair near the fire and put his cup down. He had a plate in his other hand. He tipped it slightly my way. "Is it okay if I have this chocolate cake? I haven't eaten for hours."

"Help yourself. There's plenty. You know what Erin's like, she always makes too much."

Using a fork, Seb shovelled a big chunk of the cake into his mouth. With his cheeks full, he said, "How's Erin doing? How's her pregnancy progressing?"

"She's taking things a bit easier, at last." I smiled at Seb. "A bit too easy. She's even bossier now. She gives me orders from the minute we meet in the morning and doesn't stop all day. If I could go to the toilet for her, I'm sure she'd have me doing that too. But I shouldn't complain. I'm more concerned about her health than my feelings."

Another bit of cake went into Seb's mouth. He waved his fork at me. "Tell me about the craft evening. I read Peggy's post yesterday and she said she's going to put a video up following the event. I'll have to watch it later."

I cradled the cup some more. The heat was taking the pain away from my fingers. I told Seb about the rest of the evening, as much as I could remember before I'd taken myself away from all the action.

Seb finished his cake and put the plate down. He came over to the sofa and sat next to me. "Can I have a look at the pattern, please?"

"You can."

Seb picked it up and looked at the front cover. "This model looks like one of those film stars from the 1950s. Mum loves those old films. I don't mind them either." A faraway look came into his eyes. "Falling in love seemed so much easier in those days. There weren't as many complications. A man and a woman met, they fell in love, got married and lived happily ever after." He shook his head as if to clear his thoughts. "You don't get many films like that now. It's all zombies and the end of the world." He placed the pattern on my knee.

I cast him a smile. "I didn't know you were such a romantic, Sebastian Parker."

"I'm not. I'm a hard-hearted, tough-talking man of the law. I have steel in my eyes and titanium in my heart. Do you want a hand with that knitting? Or another cup of tea?"

"Can you knit?" I asked.

He lifted his chin. "I can. Don't sound so surprised. Knitting is not just for women." He dropped his chin. "I'm useless at crocheting, though. How far have you got with your pattern?"

I finished the tea and put my cup down. "I've done the back and front of the jumper. And one sleeve. I should have the other sleeve done soon, and then I'll sew them up."

"I can sew the completed pieces together. That'll save you a bit of time."

I gave him a surprised look. "Are you sure? Don't you want to go home and get some sleep?"

"Not yet. Pass me your completed pieces. Where's your darning needle?"

I handed everything to Seb and he got to work on sewing the pieces together. I returned to my knitting work on the sleeve.

We chatted amiably over the next hour as we worked. I told Seb how the building work was coming along at the café. He talked about his work at the police station. It was lovely to have company. Seb was easy to talk to.

I was so engrossed in my knitting that I didn't realise Seb had fallen asleep until I heard him snore. His head was resting on the back of the sofa and his hands were on the almost-finished jumper on his knee. I didn't have the heart to wake him.

I completed the casting-off row on the sleeve and put it down on the table in front of me. I carefully lifted Seb's hands and retrieved the jumper. I put that on the table too.

I shuffled down in the sofa and rested my head on the cushions. My eyes were stinging with tiredness. I decided to rest them for a while before I resumed knitting. My throbbing fingers needed a rest too.

It seemed like minutes later that Seb was calling my name. I opened my eyes and was surprised to find his arms wrapped around me.

He looked into my eyes, concern etched on his face. He said softly, "Karis, what did you see? You've been crying non-stop for the last ten minutes."

I blinked at him and tried to recall the vision which had invaded my dream. It came back to me and I mumbled, "He didn't turn up. I waited and waited. But he never showed."

"Who didn't?" Seb released me and handed me a tissue.

I took it and wiped my cheeks. I was surprised at how wet they were. I said, "I was standing in the high street. Opposite the supermarket. But it looked different. The cars looked different too. They were old-fashioned, but they looked new. I was waiting for someone." I looked towards the jumper on the table. "I was wearing my new twin set. I was excited. I knew he would like it." I frowned as I looked back at Seb. "But he didn't turn up. My heart felt like it was breaking."

"It sounds like you were stood up. Could you see the woman who was wearing the twin set?"

My frown increased. "No. This is weird. Normally, I experience visions as if I'm standing nearby and watching. I'm never part of the vision. This time, it was different. I felt as if I was reliving everything that went on. Every emotion and every thought. But why? I don't understand why I'm getting these visions."

"We can work that out," Seb said. "I don't have to be at work for hours. I'll nip home and get a shower. When I come back, we'll go to that area on the high street where you had this latest vision. You might pick up on anything there. You should take the completed jumper with you."

"I haven't finished sewing the other sleeve on yet."

Seb gave me a small grin. "I did that while you were asleep. I've made you a cup of tea too." He stood up. "I won't be long. I'll let myself out."

"Seb, you don't have to do this. I can go on my own."

"Nonsense. I'm coming with you. I like a good mystery. I want to see where this one is going. See you soon."

He walked out of the room and I heard the front door opening. I then heard an indignant voice aimed at Seb.

Seb replied, "I don't have time to chat, Peggy. Bye."

Peggy came rushing into the room. "Karis Booth! Have you been up to shenanigans with DCI Parker?"

I bristled. "I certainly have not."

"His car has been parked outside all night. What's going on?"

"Nothing's going on. Well, something's been going on, but not what you think. Sit down and I'll tell you everything."

Peggy sat next to me and I told her about my latest vision. I also told her how Seb had helped me with the jumper.

She nodded. "That's a good idea of Seb's to visit the scene. I wish I could come with you, but I've got my blog to catch up on. You should see how many comments I've got to reply to. The internet waits for no woman." She patted my knee and then stood up. "Let me know how you get on."

"Peggy, I'd like to know where this twin set pattern came from. I feel it's important. Would you be able to find out, please?"

"I'll try. I'll send a message to Jade and ask her where she got those patterns from. I know she mentioned charity shops, but I'll see if she can narrow it down." She gave me a long look. "Karis, if you're going to have men staying over every night, you should get them to park their cars down a side road so the neighbours don't know they're here."

"I wasn't planning on having men staying over," I argued.

"And you should get them to leave by the back door. Perhaps they should wear a disguise so no one recognises them. You know what people are like around here. They're always poking their noses into other people's business. Not like me. I keep myself to myself."

I said with a smile, "I know you do."

Peggy continued, "But if you are going to have more male visitors, keep your curtains tightly closed. You don't want any nosy nellies peeping through and seeing things they shouldn't."

I shook my head in exasperation. "I won't be having any more male visitors."

"Not even Seb Parker?"

"Well, yes, Seb might come back. But he's just a friend."

Peggy gave me a firm nod. "Make sure he stays that way. Seb's eyes twinkle far too much when he looks at you. I've noticed that. Don't let him bewitch you with his twinkles."

"I won't."

Peggy gave me another knowing look before leaving the house. I had a quick shower and a rushed breakfast before Seb returned.

As I opened the door to him a short while later, I did notice the twinkle in his eyes. It was a nice twinkle. A friendly twinkle. It couldn't be anything but a friendly twinkle, not between Seb and me. We were friends. That's all.

# Chapter 5

My good friend, Seb, drove us the short distance to the high street. We parked up and walked down the street until we came to the area where I'd experienced my vision.

I stopped and looked at the supermarket across the road. It was the same well-known company that had been around for years.

Seb noticed me looking that way and said, "This supermarket has been here for as long as I can remember. That doesn't help us to narrow down the year your vision took place. Can you remember what the cars looked like in your vision? It could give us an indication of which time frame we're looking at."

I grimaced. "I'm not very good when it comes to recognising cars. I don't know whether they were from the 1950s or later."

"Hang on a mo." Seb took his phone out and tapped on it. He showed me the screen. "Do these look familiar?"

I shook my head.

He brought other images up and showed me them.

I tilted my head. "Sort of. But not exactly."

"Let me try another one. Here. Look at this image."

I peered at the screen. "Yes, they do look more like the cars I saw. What year was that photo taken?"

"1958. I think the style of that twin set could have come from around that era. Are you getting any visions now? Are you getting any tingly feelings? Do you need to close your eyes?"

I looked up and down the street. "Nothing's coming to me yet." I closed my eyes and brought to mind the image I'd experienced just before I woke up this morning.

Nothing.

I opened my eyes and looked at the building behind me. It was a bargain shop, and it had everything you need, and didn't need, for less than £2.

I said to Seb, "Do you know what was here before this shop?"

"It's been many things. I remember it being a charity shop, and then a clothes shop. I'm sure Peggy would know. So would my mum. I'll make some enquiries. Do you want to have a go at your vision again?"

"I'm not getting anything." I suddenly let out a sigh of exasperation. "I forgot to bring the pattern with me! And the jumper too! I meant to put them in my bag."

"It's okay. We can go back for them now." Seb's phone rang. He answered it and turned slightly away from me. He mumbled something to whoever was calling him.

He ended the call and put his phone away. "Sorry, Karis, I have to go to the station immediately. We can do this later. I'll give you a lift home."

"No, don't be silly. It's not far. I'll walk. I could do with the fresh air."

"Are you sure? I don't mind. I want to help you."

"You've already helped me. Off you go."

"I'll phone you later. Let me know if you have any other visions."

"I will."

He gave me a nod of farewell and swiftly walked away.

I stayed where I was. It was sometimes easier to have visions when I was on my own. I took a deep breath and softened my focus. I thought about the previous view of the supermarket I'd seen. I brought up the memory of the cars too.

New feelings washed over me.

My shoulders dropped. My heart. My aching heart. It was hurting so much.

The scenery around me didn't alter, but my feelings intensified. Then they changed.

The ache from my heart vanished. Sweat broke out on my forehead. My pulse quickened. I could sense danger. I swallowed and tried to control my breaths which were coming too quickly.

"Excuse me, love, are you alright?"

I jumped at the woman who was standing next to me.

"Are you having a funny turn, love?" she continued. "You've gone all white and still. Are you one of those human statutes? Those people who stand still for hours and then suddenly move. Are you one of them? Have you got a collection pot somewhere? I can give you a pound." She began to search her handbag.

I found my voice. "No, sorry. I'm not a statue. Sorry." I flashed her a smile before quickly walking away. The feelings of being in danger had passed, but I hadn't forgotten how intense they'd been.

I returned home and found Peggy sitting on the sofa in my front room. We had keys to each other's houses, so I wasn't surprised to see her there.

She took one look at my face and said, "Something's happened, hasn't it? Sit down and tell me everything. I hope you don't mind, but I've made a start on the cardigan part of your twin set." She pointed to the knitting at her side. "The sooner we get this done, the better."

"Thanks, Peggy." I sat next to her and told her about the feelings I'd experienced. I concluded, "Whoever was standing in the high street all those years ago is in danger." I thought about my words. "Or was in danger. I don't know if I'm getting feelings from the past or the future."

Peggy resumed her knitting. "We could be dealing with an unsolved murder. The woman who owned this pattern could have been brutally murdered years ago, and her murderer is walking around scot-free. Well, not for long they won't. Not with us on the case." She finished the row and switched the work to her other hand. "Excuse the pun, but on the other hand, we could be looking at a murder which is yet to occur."

"That's what I was thinking too." I watched Peggy's hands as they whizzed through the row she was working on. She wasn't even looking at it. I said, "I suspect I'll get another vision when this twin set is completed. I'll make a start on the sleeves."

I found another set of knitting needles and got to work. I was much slower than Peggy, but I kept going.

We put the TV on and watched a couple of detective shows while we clicked away on our needles. We stopped now and again for refreshments and the chance to stretch our fingers.

Thanks to the super speedy knitter at my side, the twin set was completed by late afternoon.

Peggy sewed it up and then handed it to me reverently.

I put the the jumper part of the twin set on first. It was a snug fit, but Peggy assured me that's how they were worn back in the day.

With trepidation, I put the cardigan on over the jumper. I smoothed it down and looked at Peggy.

She stood up and said, "You don't want me gawping at you while you concentrate. I'll leave you to it. I'll be in the kitchen if you need me."

"Thanks, Peggy." I could already hear a buzzing in my ears which indicated a vision was on its way. My scalp prickled with a mixture of fear and excitement. This was going to be a strong vision.

# Chapter 6

The vision came to me.

I was standing opposite the supermarket again. Thanks to the images Seb had shown me, I could now identify the cars driving past me as being from the 1950s. A glance up and down the street showed people wearing clothes from that era.

I looked down at my own attire and smiled when I saw I was wearing the blue twin set. I touched my neck and felt the presence of a pearl necklace.

I jumped as I felt a hand on my arm. A rosy-cheeked young woman was standing at my side. She seemed familiar to the woman whose memories I was experiencing. The young woman looked me up and down and said, "Hi! You look cool in that outfit! How long have you been waiting here for him?"

I checked my watch. I felt a stirring of disappointment as I said, "Twenty minutes. I'm sure he'll be here soon."

The young woman made a face of disapproval. "It should be him waiting for you. He's lucky to have you. I'll tell him that the next time I see him. I'm meeting Bob inside. Do you want to wait with us in there?"

I shook my head and forced a smile on my face. "He won't be long. He'll be here soon. I know he will. He won't let me down." I tugged on the hem of my cardigan. "Do you really think I look okay in this? It's not too glamorous is it?"

The woman beamed. "You look like a star. If you change your mind, we'll be inside." She turned away and walked towards the building behind me.

I wanted to see what the building was, but my vision wouldn't allow it.

I waited and waited. With every minute that passed, my heart felt heavier. I was aware of couples walking past and giving me sympathetic looks. It was obvious I was waiting for someone. It was just as obvious that I'd been stood up.

My eyes prickled as I finally accepted the truth. He wasn't going to turn up. He didn't care about me. He'd been lying to me for months. He said he loved me. But he didn't. He wouldn't treat me like this if he loved me.

I felt tears rolling down my cheeks. The people walking by gave me a wide berth. I knew I should leave, but I couldn't. There was the smallest sliver of hope in my heart which kept my feet in place.

My tears dripped off my chin and landed on the beautiful blue twin set which I'd painstakingly created.

A soft voice called out, "Karis. Don't cry."

It was Peggy's voice. Her concerned tone brought me back to the present. I blinked and looked at Peggy's worried face. She was sitting at my side with a box of tissues on her lap.

She handed a tissue to me and said, "I didn't mean to interrupt, but I couldn't help it. Tears were streaming down your face. You looked so sad. I couldn't bear to see you like that for a moment longer. It made me too sad." Her eyes glistened. "I'm so sorry. Did I interrupt you at an important bit?"

I wiped my eyes and told Peggy what I'd seen. I said, "I thought I might get a different vision this time. But it was more of the same. The woman was waiting for someone. I tried to look at the building behind me, but I couldn't. Peggy, despite feeling so sad, I kept picking up on an element of danger. But I don't know why."

Peggy patted my hand. "It'll come to you. I've been thinking about that part of the high street and what used to be there. I don't know why I didn't think of this earlier. There used to be a cinema opposite the supermarket. It was there during the 50s and 60s. I used to go there with my Jeff." Her eyes crinkled up. "We used to canoodle on the back row. Lots of couples did."

I smiled at her cheeky expression. "That would explain why the woman I keep turning into is standing outside the building. She must have been on a date, but he didn't turn up. She felt so sad." I put my hand on my chest. "It felt like my heart was breaking in two."

Peggy frowned. "I don't understand why you're picking up feelings of danger. Did something happen to her after she left the high street? Did her date turn up later and attack her? I suppose we could look online for any suspicious deaths which occurred around that time. Or any missing people."

"We could do. Did you get a message to Jade about where she found the knitting pattern?"

"I did. She got back to me a few minutes ago. There are a few charity shops she visits regularly. She can't remember which one had the patterns, though. She said she'd go back to the shops and talk to the staff. She can't do it now because she's got university lectures for the rest of the day. I told her not to bother and said I'd go to the charity shops and make my own enquiries. I know a few people who do volunteer work at some of them." She let out a sigh. "There could be a problem."

"What sort of problem?" I asked.

"If someone brought the patterns in, a member of staff might remember who it was. But if the patterns came via a street collection, then they won't know who donated them. Karis, I'm not hopeful that I'll find any useful information, but I'll try. Do you want to come with me? You might have a funny feeling while we're in one of the shops."

"That's a good idea." I looked down at my twin set which was slightly damp with my tears. "I'll keep this on. It might help."

There was a knock at the door. Peggy went over to the door and opened it.

A moment later, Seb came into the room.

He gave me a worried look. "Karis, have you been crying?"

I flapped my hand in a dismissive manner. "It's nothing. I'm fine. Have you got some information for us?"

"I have. I've discovered the building on the high street used to be a cinema." He smiled proudly.

Peggy said, "I've already told Karis that. I used to go there with my Jeff."

Seb's smile died. "Oh, right. I shouldn't have bothered checking online. I should have asked you."

"Yes, you should. What else have you found out?" Peggy asked him.

Seb's chest puffed out ever so slightly. "The cinema was closed in the early 70s. The building is still there, of course. However, some of the cinema's fittings have been saved."

Hope bubbled up inside me. "Fittings? What kind of fittings?"

"Some of the seats and film reels. A local cinema enthusiast bought them. He converted his shed into a small cinema. I've been in touch with him. He said he can open the cinema for us." Seb looked uncertain. "Karis, would that help you if we went to the cinema? I don't want to assume anything."

I gave him an enthusiastic nod. "It would help! I know it would. I'm already getting excited about going there." I stood up. "Can we go now?"

Seb's gaze travelled up and down my twin set. He cleared his throat and said, "You finished it. You look very nice in it." He cleared his throat again. "Very glamorous."

Peggy tutted and said, "Put your eyes back in your sockets, Seb Parker. Don't look at Karis as if she's a piece of meat."

Seb blustered, "I'm not! I wasn't!"

Peggy chuckled. "I'm only kidding. You can't help yourself. You're just a man."

I suddenly remembered something. "Oh, Peggy, I said I'd go to the charity shops with you."

"That doesn't matter," she said. "I can go on my own. You go to the cinema with this eager young man." She turned to face Seb full on and wagged a finger at him. "You behave yourself. You're an officer of the law."

Seb replied, "Of course I'll behave myself. What do you think I'm going to do?"

A wistful look came into Peggy's eyes. She said wistfully, "I know what I'd do in that cinema if my Jeff was still alive."

Seb stared at her in shock and held his hand up. "I don't want the details."

Peggy chuckled. "Are you sure? I don't mind sharing my memories."

Seb looked at me. "Karis, are you ready to go now?"

I smiled at the pleading tone in his voice. "I'm ready."

# Chapter 7

The cinema enthusiast was an elderly man called Charles. He must have been in his nineties. His voice was quiet as he welcomed us to his property. On unsteady legs, he took us to the large shed at the bottom of his garden.

When we reached the shed, Charles put a wrinkly hand on the door to steady himself. He wheezed while he got his breath back. He looked as if a stiff breeze could knock him to his knees. I noticed Seb's hands were raised at his sides to catch Charles if he suddenly keeled over.

Charles produced a key from a long chain around his neck and announced, "Good evening to you both. I will be showing a variety of films tonight for your pleasure." He stopped for breath again. A whistling sound came from his throat. He continued, "I will provide refreshments during the intervals. If you need to use the public conveniences, please ring the bell at the rear of the cinema and I will escort you to the nearest bathroom." He wheezed and whistled again. "Which is in my house."

He somehow managed to get the key into the lock. The door swung open and Charles went with it. Seb dashed forward and caught the old man before he collapsed to the floor.

Charles said, "I do apologise for the inconvenience that my advanced years are causing. My spirit is willing, but my body is refusing to cooperate." He gave Seb a smile. "Thank you for catching me, young sir. Please, make your way to the nearest available seats.

The first film will begin shortly." He wobbled towards a curtained-off area at the back of the interior.

Seb whispered, "Do you think he's okay? I didn't realise he was so old when I spoke to him on the phone."

"We'll keep an eye on him." I looked around the shed. "Seb, look at this. Isn't it lovely? Look at all the fittings. They must be years old."

There were three rows of seats. Each row had four connecting chairs. The chairs were made of dark wood and had upholstered cushions made of red velvet. The colour on the lower cushions was a paler shade of red. I smiled as I thought about how many local shuffling bottoms had sat in these seats. A huge screen covered the front wall. There was something on a small table at the side of the screen.

I pointed it out to Seb and said, "You don't think he's going to play that, do you?"

Seb broke into a smile. "I think he just might." He crooked his elbow at me. "Shall we take a seat?"

We sat in the middle row, and in the middle seats. We heard some shuffling noises in the curtained-off area, along with some wheezing and whistling.

A few minutes later, we heard Charles shuffling down the aisle. He'd changed into a three-piece suit complete with bow tie. He waved a torch from side to side as he went even though he didn't need to. He settled himself on a stool in front of the item which I'd pointed out to Seb. He pushed his sleeves up and then began to play the small keyboard in front of him. A jaunty tune boomed out.

I gripped Seb's arm and whispered, "Isn't this wonderful? It's like we've gone back in time."

Seb winced. "I appreciate the musical effect, but he's not the most accomplished player, is he? I hope he doesn't go on too long."

Charles played for a few more minutes. Then he got to his feet and gave us an unsteady bow. I burst into applause. Seb clapped too, but not as enthusiastically as me.

Charles wobbled away from the keyboard and back up the aisle. He stopped to rest at the end of our row and put his hand on the nearest chair. He huffed, "The film will begin shortly."

"Do you need a hand?" Seb offered.

"No, thank you. I'll be okay in a second or two." He huffed a bit more and then wobbled away.

Seb said to me, "I feel guilty about asking him to do this for us now. Is being here having any effect on you?"

I nodded. "Something is happening to me. I can sense a vision coming my way. I usually get a buzzing in my ears first, and that's happening now. Seb, if you see me crying, don't stop me. I have to experience every emotion that comes to me."

He gave me an uncertain look. "Okay."

The lights dimmed and the screen lit up. The image of a film company's logo appeared on the screen. Music blared out. My stomach flipped in excitement.

The film began. It was a black and white one from the 1950s. I'd seen this one with Mum years ago. Just like Seb's mum, she loved watching old films.

As the film continued, the shed vanished from around me. I was now sitting in a large cinema and it was full of people. The same film was playing on the huge screen.

I was holding hands with someone at my side. I glanced that way and saw a young man with combed-back hair. My heart swelled with love for him. It was the same man who'd flittered into my mind when I'd first started knitting the twin set.

He looked my way, smiled and moved his head closer. He whispered, "Those Hollywood women are not a patch on you. You're much more beautiful." He planted a soft kiss on my cheek.

I felt my cheeks warming up and my heart filled with more love. I felt so safe in the presence of this young man. He was my world. My everything.

My attention briefly went to the screen and I noticed what the main character was wearing. I whispered to the young man, "Do you think a twin set like that would suit me?"

His eyes shone with love as he answered, "You would look even more beautiful. I'd love to see you in something like that."

I gave him a nod. "Then I'll knit myself one. I'll wear it when we next come here."

He squeezed my hand and turned his face back to the screen.

My head was full of thoughts about where I could get the pattern from. I could try the market but I doubted they'd have anything as glamorous as the twin set the film star was wearing. Could I send off for one? I'd have a look in Mum's magazines.

I was so lost in my thoughts that I didn't notice the scenery around me changing.

I jumped as an older man appeared in front of me and shouted, "You hurt him! You killed him! I know you did!" He lunged and put his hands around my throat. He snarled, "You'll pay for what you did!"

One of my hands clawed at the man as I tried to push him away. My other hand scrambled at my side until I located what I was searching for. I grabbed the metal item and thrust it towards the man. It connected with him and—

"Karis! Karis!" Seb was shaking me by the shoulders.

I focused on his face and realised I was back in the shed. My throat felt sore.

Seb still had his hands on my shoulders. He said, "I know you told me not to interfere, but I had to for your own safety. You had your hand around your neck. You were struggling to breathe."

I put a hand on my throat. "Was I?"

He nodded. "You were screaming and yelling. You were waving your other hand in the air. What happened? What did you see?"

I quickly told Seb about the young man in the cinema. I explained, "When that vision faded, I was in a room in a house. I didn't take it in much, so I can't describe it. The man who was shouting at me looked like an older version of the young man. I think it was him. He had the same eyes. He was going to kill me." I paused as I recalled the weapon which had been used on the older man. "The woman he was attacking stabbed him with a knitting needle. She thrust it into his neck." I abruptly stopped and began to tremble. "I could feel it going into him."

Seb pulled me into his arms and patted my back. "It's okay. It's all over now."

I looked up at him. "But it isn't over. I have to stop this happening. I could feel every emotion the woman was feeling. She didn't want to hurt that man. As soon as she did so, she was overcome with guilt. I can't let that happen to her."

Seb released me. "But didn't you say the older man accused her of killing someone?"

I nodded. "I don't think she did kill anyone. She was shocked when he said that. Really shocked." I lowered my head. "I have to find her somehow."

Seb put his hand over mine. "I'll help you."

Charles wheezed as he shuffled towards us. "Is everything alright? I heard the young lady screaming. Do you need some smelling salts? I've got some in the kitchen which belonged to Mother. It won't take me long to get them."

Seb stood up and said, "No, thank you. The young lady is okay. Thank you very much for your time. I'm afraid we have to go now."

Charles' face dropped. "That's a shame. I've got another film lined up."

I moved closer to Charles and said, "I know many people who would love to visit your wonderful cinema. Could I put your details online?"

"Online? You mean that internet thing? That one that goes all around the world?"

"Yes," I said. "My neighbour would love to come here too. She has plenty of friends who'd come along with her."

Charles wobbled on his feet. Seb put his hand out and steadied the elderly gent. Charles smiled. "That would be wonderful. Truly wonderful. You have my sincere thanks. Let me see you to the exit door. Watch your step as you go."

As soon as we got into Seb's car, I checked my phone. There was a message from Peggy. She needed to see me as soon as possible.

# Chapter 8

Seb dropped me off outside Peggy's house. He said, "As much as I'd love to know what's so urgent, I have to get back to the station. Karis, will you keep me up to date with this knitting pattern mystery?"

I heard the concern in his voice. "Course I will. Why do you sound so worried?"

"It's the mention of murder. I don't want you putting yourself in danger." His brow furrowed. "When I get back to the station, I'll make some enquiries about knitting-related accidents or murders. If I find anything, I'll let you know."

"Thanks, Seb. And thanks for taking my visions so seriously."

"Thank you for letting me know about them." He gave me a soft smile. It abruptly left his face as someone rapped on my window. Seb lowered the window and Peggy pushed her head through.

She snapped, "Don't sit there chatting like you've got all the time in the world. Come inside. I've got something to tell you." Her eyes narrowed as she gave Seb the once over. "Did you keep your hands to yourself in that cinema shed?"

"I did," Seb told her solemnly.

Peggy opened the door and said to me, "Come on, Karis. Seb, are you coming in too?"

"No. I have to get back to the station."

"Fair enough," Peggy said.

As soon as I got out of the car, Peggy closed the door and waggled her fingers in goodbye at Seb. She took me by the elbow and marched me up the path. I looked over at Seb and managed to get a smile out before he drove away.

Peggy took me into the kitchen. I moved towards the chairs.

"Don't sit down," she ordered. "I want to take some photos of you."

"Me? What for?"

Peggy picked her phone up and squinted at the screen. "It's not so much you as the twin set you're wearing. I've got a plan." She looked back at me and raised the camera. "Stand up straight. Don't move." I heard the noise of a photo being taken. Peggy continued, "Turn to the side. Look straight ahead. You don't need to smile as I'm not including your face."

I turned to the side and grumbled, "I feel like you're taking police shots of me. Shouldn't there be a height chart behind me?"

Peggy chuckled. "Turn around. Let me get a back view now. I'll share my plan with you when I've done this."

She took a few more photos and then allowed me to sit down.

I took a seat and said, "How did you get on at the charity shops?"

She shook her head in disgust and took the seat opposite me. "Not very well. A lot of the staff I saw were young volunteers. Miserable as sin, they were. Why do volunteer work if you're going to stand there with a face like a slapped fish?" She tutted.

"A slapped fish?"

Peggy nodded. "When I do volunteer work, I'm happy as Larry. Whoever Larry is. I knew a Larry once. He was a misery guts. Never cracked a smile in all the years I'd known him. Mind you, if I looked like him, I never would have smiled too. He had this weird-looking nose and his eyes were—"

"Peggy," I interrupted her, "what did you find out at the charity shops?"

"I was just getting to that," Peggy said indignantly. "I went to all the shops that Jade visited and none of them knew anything about knitting patterns. To be honest, they didn't know much about anything. That's beside the point. The young fella in the last shop was slightly less useless than the other assistants. He thinks a bunch of patterns came into the shop last week. But he's not certain.

His manager is in tomorrow and he said she might know more. So, we'll go there tomorrow."

"Okay." I looked at her phone. "Why were you taking photos of me?"

She lifted her chin and proclaimed, "Being an online entrepreneur has taught me many lessons. The main one is that people spend far too much time online. If you want to know an answer to a question, you should post your query online and see who crawls out of the woodwork to answer it."

"Woodwork? Peggy, you're full of sayings today. What question are you going to post online?"

"I'm getting to that. I'm only going to put it on my blog for my readers. I don't want just anyone looking at it." She raised her phone. "I'm going to put these photos on my blog along with a picture of the pattern. I'll ask if anyone knows where the pattern could have come from. Or if they have any relatives or friends who could have knitted this twin set in the 1950s. Whoever knitted it could still be alive. I'll mention the cinema and the year too. It's a long shot, but you never know. There are some very nosy people in this town." Her confident look wavered. "Is that the kind of information you need? Would it help to narrow down who could have used that pattern?"

I gave her a nod. "Considering her life is in danger, it would help a lot."

Peggy put her phone down. "In danger? What do you mean? Tell me everything."

I told her about my latest visions.

Peggy leaned back in her chair and surmised, "So, the mystery knitter could have killed someone in the past. And now the past has come back to haunt her in the shape of that older man. Is she going to kill again? Or has she already committed the dastardly deed?"

"I don't know."

"Is she the one you're supposed to help?"

"I don't know."

"Or are you supposed to help the victim before he gets impaled on a knitting needle?"

I shrugged. "I don't know that either."

Peggy nodded to herself. "This knitter of yours could be a serial killer. She could have been bumping off people for years. And now she's masquerading as a feeble old woman. That's a good disguise. No one would ever suspect an old woman of being up to no good."

I gave her a pointed look but didn't say anything.

Peggy was lost in her thoughts now. "I wonder where she puts the bodies? Do you think she kills them all with knitting needles? She'll have to use the thicker ones to do a proper job. There's no point using a thin one. It would only snap. Perhaps it was trial and error for her to begin with. Maybe she tried other weapons first. A crochet hook perhaps?"

"Peggy," I called out to her, "can we talk about something else? I don't want to think about our knitter as a killer. I didn't pick up on any murderous feelings in my visions."

Peggy gave me a wise look. "That's because she would have justified her actions. That's what criminal masterminds do. I read a book from the library about that. Put the kettle on and I'll post these photos online. I'm sure we'll have some replies soon. Whether those replies will be any use is another matter."

I stood up, moved over to the kettle and filled it up. Once I'd switched it on, I said to Peggy, "I'm going to change out of this twin set."

She gave me a knowing look. "Is it because you're picking up feelings of guilt about slaying so many people?"

I gave her a long look. "No, it isn't that at all. To be honest, I feel scared. Not just a bit scared, but thoroughly petrified. Something awful is going to happen to our mystery knitter soon."

# Chapter 9

Despite my anxious feelings, I managed to get a decent night's sleep. When I woke up, I checked my phone for messages. There was one from Erin to say she was already at the café and she would meet me there soon. One from Peggy informed me she was working on some leads, but she didn't want to tell me what those were in a message. She added that she had some volunteer work to do at the local hospital and would meet me later.

I shook my head at Peggy's words. I didn't know where she got her energy from.

There weren't any messages from Seb, so I presumed that was a good thing.

After showering and having my breakfast, I headed over to the café. I found Erin and Robbie in the kitchen. The radio was on and they were dancing with each other. Erin looked radiant and my heart filled with love for her.

Even though Robbie had his back to me as he wiggled his ample hips, he said to Erin, "Don't look now, but I think we're being watched. I think it's one of those voyeur types. We should charge her if she's going to stare at us." He chuckled, looked over his shoulder at me and winked.

"I've only been standing here for a few moments," I defended myself. "You two make such a lovely couple."

"I know," Robbie said. He held his hand out to Erin. She took it and Robbie twirled her gently around and then wrapped his arms around her.

Erin laughed and freed herself. "That's enough messing about, Robbie. We're supposed to be getting the café ready." She picked something off the counter and came over to me. "Karis, the new menus have arrived. They look great. Have a look."

I took the menu and studied it. "I love the colours. The font is good too."

Erin tapped the top of the menu. "I'm still not happy about keeping the old name. I think we should incorporate both our names. You've put loads of money into this business. You should get the recognition."

I gave her the menu back. "It's been called Erin's Café for years. You've already built up a reputation. I'm not going to mess with that. Do we know when the café can reopen?" I sent Robbie an eager look.

Robbie cleared his throat and announced, "In my humble opinion, the café should be ready for opening next week."

Erin pulled the menu to her chest and her eyes shone with excitement. "Next week, Karis, next week! Can you believe it? There will have to be a grand reopening, of course. We'll put posts on our website. What about an opening day discount? Should we do that? We could have half-price cakes or something. We have to do something special. We have to celebrate the reopening." Her voice rose and the peaceful look on her face fled.

I put my hand on her arm. "I've already thought of that. I'll show you my plans later. Everything's under control. You don't have to worry. In fact, all you have to do is bake those wonderful cakes of yours."

Erin took a deep breath. "Thank you. I don't know what I'd do without you." She gave me a long look. "What's going on with you and that knitting pattern you were so excited about? Have you had any more visions?"

I gave her a half-shrug. "It's nothing important."

"Of course it's important. I want to know everything." Her eyes narrowed. "Have you witnessed a murder?"

Robbie called over, "If you're going to talk about murders, do it while you're sitting down. Erin, take Karis over to the table by the window. I'll bring you both a latte over. I'm going to have another go at that coffee machine. It's not going to get the better of me. It's man versus machine. And this man is going to be victorious." He gave us a nod to add conviction to his words.

Erin and I left the kitchen and took a seat at the table next to the window. The window was covered with paper as we didn't want anyone to see the inside of the café until it was finished. We took a moment to admire the table and chairs we'd taken so long to decide on buying.

I told Erin what I'd experienced in my visions so far. Her eyebrows rose at the mention of Seb's name. Thankfully, she didn't say anything.

When I'd finished, Erin said, "So, what are you going to do now?"

"I want to find out who the knitting pattern belonged to. If she's still alive, that is. Peggy's got some leads. I don't know what those are. I'll speak to her soon about that."

Robbie came over to the table. He had a defeated look on his face. He put two cups down and said forlornly, "It's tea. The coffee machine got the better of me. There are too many levers and buttons on it."

Erin said, "Don't give up. You can do this. Have another go."

He lifted his chin. "I will do. I'll sneak up on it when it's not looking. Do you want any cake?"

"Yes, please!" Peggy announced as she came through the door. She smiled at us. "I thought I'd find you lot here. Robbie, I'll have whatever Erin and Karis are having to drink. As long as it's not coffee. It's too early in the morning for coffee." She came over to us, pulled a chair out and sat down. She looked up at Robbie. "I'll have some cake if Erin's made it. If you've made it, I'll have a chocolate biscuit instead."

Robbie tipped his head at Peggy, gave Erin and me a smile, and ambled away.

Peggy began, "Erin, has Karis got you up to speed with her visions?"

"She has."

"Good. And how are you feeling today?"

"I feel great," Erin said.

"Good. Let's get down to business. Karis, I've had some comments about those photos I posted last night of you in that twin set." Her face twisted in disgust. "Some of the comments were quite inappropriate."

"In what way?" I asked.

"Certain people made remarks about your lovely figure. I won't go into details. I won't have comments like that on my blog. I gave those people a piece of my mind, and then I blocked them from making any future comments." She shook her head and added a tut of disgust. "Anyway, I did get the names of women who could have owned that pattern. Through one source and another, I've narrowed down who is of the right age, and if they lived in this area when that cinema was open. My readers have been extremely helpful, and I've managed to get the names and addresses of three potential knitters. I don't know whether these women can help us, but it's a start. We can call on them later."

I stared at Peggy in amazement. "That's great news. This must have taken you hours. When did you do this?"

"I was up early. You know I like to make an early start in the day." She smiled at us. "When you haven't got many days left in your life, you need to make the most of every minute."

Erin said, "Don't talk like that, Peggy. I want you to be around for at least the next forty years."

"Sorry, love," Peggy said. "I didn't mean to upset you. Old people like to talk about death. You should hear how some of my friends natter on about it. Back to the problem at hand. Look what I found." She reached into her big bag and pulled out a stack of knitting patterns. She put them on the table. "These are the patterns that Jade brought in the other night. Karis, there could be something here that could help you. Have a good look at them."

Robbie returned with a cup of tea and a slice of cake for Peggy. "Here you go, madam." He put them on the table.

Peggy said, "Where's the cake for your wife? And your sister-in-law? I don't think much of the service in here. I won't be leaving you a tip."

Robbie replied, "I've already got something nutritious cooking in the oven for my wife. And as for leaving me a tip, Peggy Marshall, I'll have you know—"

I interrupted his words. "Look! Look at this one." I held up a pattern for a man's jumper. "This has got the same pencilled ring as my twin set pattern. You can see how the circle doesn't line up. These must have belonged to the same woman." I continued to look through the patterns and soon found some more.

Peggy and Erin helped me. We located ten patterns for men's jumpers which had pencilled-rings on them.

Peggy said, "I can't find any more women's patterns with the pencil marks on them. Our mystery knitter must have given up making things for herself. You know what we have to do now, Karis."

I gave her a slow nod. "We have to knit these jumpers and see if I get another vision from them. It's going to take a while." I looked at Robbie. "I'm going to need that cake. Just bring the whole thing out."

Peggy shook her head. "We don't have time to do this. I'm going to call in the cavalry."

# Chapter 10

Forty minutes later, three elderly women came into the café with determined looks on their faces and heavy bags hanging from their arms.

One of them looked at Peggy and said, "Where do you want us?"

"Over here, Celia. Thanks for coming here so quickly."

Celia nodded. "Anything for you, Peg. You said it was a knitting emergency?"

"It certainly is. I've got ten patterns for men's jumpers. They need knitting up as soon as possible. Keep to the size that's been circled on the pattern. I don't expect you to finish them all. I'll get on with some myself later."

Celia said, "We can do that. We've cancelled our social engagements for the day." She raised her bag. "We've brought supplies with us. Tea. Lemonade. Sandwiches. Medication. We can stay here all day."

"Thanks, Celia. I appreciate it."

Celia moved a bit closer and inclined her head in Peggy's direction. "Can you tell us what this is about? Or is it top secret?"

Peggy gave her a knowing look. "I'd rather not say at the moment, Celia. I hope you understand."

"Say no more, Peg, say no more. Mum's the word. Right, where should we set up camp?" She looked around the café. "I need somewhere comfy if I'm going to be sitting down all day. You know what my back's like. And I'll need to be near the toilets. My bladder's not as young as it used to be."

Erin, Robbie and I watched this exchange in stunned silence. It was like watching a well-organised army undertaking a military exercise. An army made up of pensioners in sensible clothes and comfy shoes.

Erin got to her feet and addressed the women. "There are some sofas on the other side of the café. You can sit there. The café isn't open yet, but Robbie and I would love to bring you refreshments. No charge, of course. I've made plenty of cakes, and we've got a new sandwich toaster that I'd like to try out."

Celia gave her a swift smile. "That'll be grand. But don't be on your feet too much, Erin. Not in your condition. Peg's told me about your pregnancy. Get this husband of yours to do the fetching and carrying." She looked at Robbie. "We'll have tea to begin with. We might need to move on to coffee later. How are you at making coffee? Can you make a decent one?"

"I've got a new coffee maker," Robbie told her, "but it's getting the better of me."

Celia quizzed him, "What model is it? What make is it? Does it have a frothing nozzle? What about a reheating section?"

Robbie looked dumbfounded. "I don't know."

Celia passed her bag to the woman behind her. "Jan, take this and get yourself settled in those sofas. I'd better sort this coffee situation out." She turned to Robbie and ordered, "Take me to the machine. Be quick about it. We don't have all day. Is it in the kitchen? Is it this way?" She marched towards the kitchen.

Peggy nudged Robbie and said, "I bet you thought I was a pain in the rear-end. Wait till you've spent a few hours with Celia. You'll soon realise what an angel I am."

Robbie gave her a weak smile and then rushed after Celia.

Peggy handed the patterns over to Jan. "Thanks again for doing this, Jan. I'll call back later."

Peggy and I left the café and got into my car. I said to her, "Where are we going now?"

"We'll call on the first possible knitter on our list. She's called Diana. She doesn't live far away."

I started the engine. "Are we going to just turn up? What are we going to say to her?"

"I've got that sorted out. I phoned each woman as soon as I worked out they could be a possible suspect. I told them we'd found a knitting pattern which could belong to them, and we'd like to return it. Of course, I didn't say anything about your visions and whatnot."

"But if they gave that pattern away to a charity, why would they want it back?"

Peggy's eyes glittered with mischief. "I told them there was something valuable inside the pattern. I didn't tell them what that was, but I hinted it could be money."

I shook my head at her and drove off.

Peggy said, "I had to think of something. We could be looking at a possible murder here."

"I know. I'm sorry. You've done so much to help me. What are we going to do when we get there? What will we say to them?"

"You leave the talking to me. All you have to do is concentrate on any emotions you pick up." She paused a fraction. "If one of them is a serial killer and they start having murderous thoughts about us, let me know."

"I will do. I hope it doesn't come to that."

We soon arrived at Diana's house. As I switched the engine off, I let out a small groan. "I haven't got the twin set pattern with me."

Peggy patted her bag. "I nipped into your house before going to the café. I've got it here."

"You think of everything," I said with a smile. "I don't know what I'd do without you."

Peggy released her seat belt. "Bear that in mind if Diana rushes towards me with a knitting needle and an evil glint in her eyes. Don't let her do away with me."

Diana was waiting at the door for us. She had grey hair and many wrinkles. Her back was stooped and her steps slow as she led us down the hallway of her bungalow. My heart lifted when I saw a knitting bag stuffed with wool at the side of her sofa. Perhaps Diana was our knitter and we would soon get to the bottom of this mystery.

"Do take a seat," Diana told us. She carefully lowered herself into an armchair, letting out a small moan as she did so.

Peggy and I sat on the sofa. Peggy took the twin set pattern out and showed it to Diana.

Peggy explained, "Thank you for seeing us at such short notice. This is the pattern I was telling you about. Do you recognise it?"

Diana squinted at the pattern through her spectacles. "I'm not sure. I had patterns like that when I was young. They were all the fashion at one stage. It was those Hollywood films, you see. We all wanted to look like those starlets." She turned the pattern over. "Ah, now then. This isn't one of mine. I never put a circle around the sizes." She looked as if she was going to say something else, but then she closed her mouth.

"Are you sure it's not one of yours?" Peggy persisted.

"I'm not absolutely certain," Diana said. "However, my sisters did borrow my knitting patterns. They could have put a circle around the numbers. It'd be something they would do. They could never keep their hands off my stuff. The cheeky blighters." She sighed heavily. "May they rest in peace." She gave the pattern back to Peggy. "Sorry, I'm not being very helpful. Would you like to stay for a tea? I haven't had any visitors for days. My son and daughter live far away, and I don't see them as much as I'd liked to. And I haven't been out to the shops for a week. Not with this cold spell in the air."

I could see the hope in Diana's eyes and said, "We can stay for a little while. Did you ever visit the cinema on the high street?"

Diana laughed. "I certainly did. I wasn't the only one. It was a magnet for couples in those days. I had my first date with my late husband there. Let me make you a cuppa and I'll tell you all about it." She let out a small moan of pain as she stood up.

Peggy got up and helped Diana to her feet. She offered, "I'll help you make the tea."

Diana gave her a smile before shuffling out of the room.

I whispered to Peggy, "She seems nice. I don't think she's the one we're looking for."

Peggy whispered back, "She could be lying through her teeth. Have a rummage about in her knitting bag. Touch her personal belongings. See if you can have a vision. Make it quick."

    She went after Diana. I didn't relish the idea of touching Diana's property, but I knew it had to be done. I reluctantly made my way over to the knitting bag and put my hands on it.

# Chapter 11

"Are you sure you didn't pick up on anything?" Peggy said as we drove away from Diana's house thirty minutes later.

"I'm sure. Diana isn't our suspect. She's just a kindly old lady."

Peggy's tone was suspicious. "Is it all an act? Has she got bodies buried in the garden? I'm not discounting her yet." Her tone brightened. "Although, she did make a super cup of tea. And I did like reminiscing about the past with her."

"Who are we seeing next?"

"A woman called Elaine. We'd better hurry up. I told her we'd be there before eleven. That Diana kept us chatting for too long."

"You did a lot of the chatting," I pointed out.

"I was gaining her trust. That's what investigators do. Turn left at this roundabout. Have you heard anything from Seb yet?"

"I haven't. I checked my phone just before we set off."

"We'll take that as good news. Take the second right."

We arrived at Elaine's house. She opened the door to us and a strong smell of perfume wafted over us. She was the total opposite of Diana. Despite being in her late years, Elaine looked radiant and full of health. She was wearing jeans and a silk shirt. A scarf was arranged elegantly around her neck. I could never get my scarves to look like that. Her face was perfectly made-up, and her hair was thick and shiny.

She gave us a warm smile of welcome and said, "I'd almost given up on you. Do come in. I'm afraid I haven't got long to talk to you. I'm going out on a date in ten minutes." She paused and her smile increased. "It's a blind date. I met him online. Have you ever tried online dating? It's a marvel. My daughter told me all about it, and she showed me which sites to go on. I've had five dates so far this month. It's an absolute hoot! Come in."

I shared a look with Peggy and then followed Elaine into her living room. It was tastefully furnished and the furniture was expensive looking. I did notice a knitting bag half-hidden behind a chair.

Elaine perched on the end of her armchair and placed her hands on her knees. Her back was straight and her look direct. She said, "Peggy, you said on the phone you might have something which belonged to me."

"I did." Peggy handed her the pattern.

Elaine smiled when she looked at the image. "This does look like something I would have made. I do like the clean lines of this twin set." Her smile grew. "I have a set of pearls just like these. They're not real, but they're good imitation ones."

"Is that your pattern?" Peggy asked.

"It might be. It might not be. Mum bought a lot of patterns for me. She insisted on me taking up knitting. She said it was a skill that would stay with me for life." She lowered the pattern. "Between you and me, I think she wanted me to spend more time at home and less time out with my friends. I was a bit of a wild one in my youth. I had many boyfriends. I used to meet them at that old cinema in town."

I leaned forward. "Was there anyone special in your life at that time?"

Elaine let out a delicate laugh. "They were all special. Until the next one came along. I thought I was in love with all of them."

Peggy spoke, "Did any of them ever stand you up outside the cinema? That happened to a friend of mine and she never got over it."

A look of anger flashed into Elaine's eyes. She said, "They wouldn't have dared stand me up." She looked at the pattern again and shook her head. "I really can't say whether this belonged to me or not. It could have been one of Mum's. Didn't you say there was something valuable with the pattern?"

"I did. It was a five-pound-note," Peggy said. As if testing Elaine for her honesty, she added, "If you think there's a fair chance the pattern belongs to you, I can give you that money."

Elaine shook her head and handed the pattern back to Peggy. "That wouldn't be honest of me as I don't know for sure if it is mine. I hope you don't think I'm being rude, but I'll have to ask you to leave. I don't want to be late for my date. Actually, I've double-booked myself today. I'm meeting two men within a short time of each other, and in the same place. I didn't think they'd both say yes to me! One of them is an old flame. I haven't seen him for years, so I couldn't say no to him."

The hairs on the back of my neck prickled. "Oh? Where are you meeting these men?"

"It's that pub just down from the supermarket in town. My old flame hasn't been here for years and that's the only building he remembers." She stood up. "I'll see you out."

As soon as we got in the car, Peggy declared, "It's her! It has to be. Did you see how angry she looked when I mentioned being stood up? And now she's going to meet an old flame! It must be the young man you saw in the cinema. It all makes sense. He's come back on the scene, and for some reason, he's going to try and kill her. But she's going to kill him instead. She's got her knitting needles ready. Did you see them?"

"I did."

"We'll have to follow her, of course. We have to stop these murders before they get going."

"How are we going to do that?" I asked. "We can't march into that pub and tell Elaine about my visions."

Peggy considered the matter. "No, we can't do that. We'll have to spy on her from afar. We'll see what happens and take it from there. If Elaine is our suspect, I wonder who else she's killed? You said the older man in your later vision accused her of murder."

"I'm not sure the woman in my vision did kill someone. The man accused her, but he didn't give any information about it. What's the name of the third woman on your list?"

"It's Martha. Is there any point calling on her now? We should be getting ourselves ready for our covert surveillance of Elaine."

"Won't Martha be expecting us?"

Peggy sighed. "She will. She sounded nice on the phone. I suppose we should turn up. I don't want to let her down. We won't stay long."

Martha welcomed us into her home and insisted on making us a drink. Once in the living room, Peggy produced the knitting pattern and asked Martha about it.

Martha examined the pattern. "I don't recognise it. It looks too fancy for me. I don't think I would have had the patience to knit that cabled part. Sorry." She handed the pattern back to Peggy.

I said to her, "Do you still knit now?"

Martha shook her head. "Not with my arthritis. I find it too painful. I used to knit for my family when I had the time." A sadness came into her eyes. "I don't need to knit for anyone now. My daughter is grown up, and my husband passed away last year."

Peggy had lost her husband a few years ago and I saw her face soften at Martha's words. Peggy said, "I'm sorry to hear that. I know how you feel. What was your husband's name?"

"Leon. He was a good husband. He did everything for me. Took good care of me and the house. He did lots of DIY." She smiled at the memory. "He was useless most of the time, but he tried."

Peggy nodded in understanding. "My Jeff was just the same. He made a mess of our home many times with his handiwork. There's a set of shelves in the spare room which have never been straight. Jeff put them up. I can't put anything on them because they slide right off. But I can't bear to take them down."

Martha said, "It's the memories, isn't it? They keep you going on a lonely night."

"Aye, they do."

Even though Peggy was anxious to leave, we stayed with Martha for a while longer and the two of them talked about their late husbands.

Peggy's eyes were watery as we headed for my car. She said, "Poor Martha. Do you think I should invite her to one of our craft evenings? It would do her good to get out of the house."

"That's a good idea." I opened the car and we got in. "Where to now?"

"Let's go to that pub where Elaine is meeting her dates." Peggy wiped her eyes. "I'll just get myself into the right frame of mind for catching a murderer. Give me a minute or two."

I checked the traffic before driving away. Peggy was unnaturally quiet as we headed into town. I hoped her conversation with Martha hadn't upset her too much. In the silence, I thought about the recent visits we'd had to the elderly women. There was something bothering me, but for the life of me, I couldn't work out what it was.

# Chapter 12

I did feel a sense of unease as Peggy and I walked into the pub where Elaine was meeting her dates. I didn't like the idea of spying on her and I voiced my concerns to Peggy.

She said, "We're here to stop a possible murder. Don't forget that." She looked around the pub. "Ah, there's Elaine over there. She's on her own. Let's get a table in the corner and watch her from there."

"Would you like a drink?" I checked my watch. "I hope they do tea and coffee. It's a bit early for something strong."

"It's never too early for a gin and tonic," Peggy said. She nodded to herself. "I should get that embroidered on a cushion. Let me give you some money for the drinks."

"No, I'll get them."

"No, I will," Peggy argued.

For the next minute, we did that ridiculous thing of both of us insisting on paying. I relented and took a ten-pound-note from Peggy. She headed off to find a table for us, and I went to the bar.

From my position at the bar, I could see Elaine. She had her back to me and I saw her looking at her watch. She was still on her own and waiting for her date. I got a gin and tonic for Peggy and a mint tea for myself. I was hoping the tea would calm my nerves. I was on edge as I cast cautious glances Elaine's way. What if she turned around and saw me staring at her? I didn't have an excuse ready as to why Peggy and I were here.

I took the drinks over to a corner table and handed the gin and tonic to Peggy. I gave her the change from her ten-pound-note.

Peggy picked her glass up and said, "I've been watching Elaine. She looks worried. Her date hasn't shown up yet. She keeps checking her phone." She took a long drink and smacked her lips together in appreciation. "That hits the spot. Karis, do you think you'll recognise the man from your vision if he turns up here?"

"I will. His face was very close to mine. I saw his features clearly."

We stopped talking as a man approached Elaine. He tapped her on the shoulder and she turned around. She looked at the man with uncertainty, to begin with, then she broke into a smile and held her hand out. The man took it and started to talk to her.

Peggy strained her neck as she looked at the couple. She muttered, "Turn around, mister. We can't see your face."

We watched in vain as Elaine and her date talked to each other. The mystery man still had his back to us.

Peggy said, "We can't see his face from here. We'll have to do something. Can you sneak over there and take a peek at his face? If you don't like the idea of doing that, I can walk past and casually take a photo of him. I can be discreet when needed."

I shook my head. "You don't need to do that. He's turned around now. It's not the man from my vision."

"Are you sure?" Peggy stood up and looked directly at the couple. Elaine and her date were now facing us as they stood at the bar.

"I'm sure."

Elaine suddenly looked Peggy's way and made direct eye contact with her. Her eyebrows rose in surprise. Then she smiled and gave Peggy a wave.

Peggy waved back and returned to her seating position. "Drat. We've been spotted. Our cover has been blown."

"It doesn't matter now. We've seen the mystery man, and he's not the one we're looking for."

"But what about the old flame? He'll be turning up soon. How are we going to take a covert look at him now that Elaine has seen us?" She shook her head. "I've let us down, Karis. I shouldn't have drawn attention to us."

I stiffened and hissed, "Elaine is coming this way."

"Act natural," Peggy hissed back. She picked her glass up, leaned back in her chair and took a big drink. She beamed as Elaine stopped at our table.

Elaine said, "Hello. I didn't think I'd see you two again, and so soon."

In a casual manner, Peggy lifted her glass and announced, "I'm having a gin and tonic. I have one every day. Sometimes two or three. I love them. When you mentioned going to the pub, I asked Karis if she would bring me here so that I could start on my favourite tipple." She laughed a bit too loudly. "It's never too early to have a gin and tonic! That's what I always say."

Elaine gave Peggy an uncertain look. "I suppose not."

I asked, "How's your date going? He looks like a friendly chap."

Elaine pulled a face. "He is friendly. Too friendly. He's already talking about us going on holiday together. He's barely let me say a word since we met. He's not my type. I'll have to make an excuse soon and leave."

Peggy offered, "Do you want me to get rid of him for you? I don't mind."

"No, thank you. I think it's best if I do it." Elaine smiled. "I've got rid of men before."

"Really?" Peggy said, "How? Did you use sharp implements on them?"

Elaine gave Peggy another uncertain look and took a step back. "Sharp implements?"

I quickly said, "Are you still going to meet your old flame?"

Elaine nodded. "I am. I can't wait to see him. But I'm not going to meet him here. He sent me a text to say he's running late. He's going to take me to a restaurant this evening instead. I don't know which one yet." She looked over at the bar. "I'd better get back to my date. I'll give him five more minutes before making my excuses." She said goodbye and walked away.

Peggy put her drink on the table and gave it a suspicious look. "How much gin is in there? It's gone straight to my head. I almost blurted out inappropriate questions to Elaine."

"You did blurt out an inappropriate question about using a sharp implement." I looked over at Elaine. She had a patient look on her face as she listened to her date. I said to Peggy, "We'll have to follow Elaine later when she goes to the restaurant."

"We will. We'll have to be more discreet next time. I suppose we'll have to hang around outside her house until she leaves." A noise came from her handbag. "Oh, that's my phone." She took her phone from her handbag and tapped on it. She said, "It's from Celia. A couple of the knitted jumpers are ready at the café."

"Already? That was quick."

"Celia doesn't mess about when it comes to knitting. We can't do anything else here. Let's go and have a look at those jumpers. With a bit of luck, you might have another vision." She stared at her half-full glass and then heaved a big sigh. "I'm not going to drink the rest of it. I need to keep a clear head. Come on, Karis, let's go before I change my mind and down this drink in one."

Peggy swiftly stood up and walked away. She waved to Elaine on the way out.

I looked Elaine's way and saw the discomfort on her face as the man in front of her chatted away. He was standing too close to her and seemed almost aggressive. I made a flash decision and headed over to her.

I announced loudly, "Elaine! I thought it was you." I pulled her into a hug and whispered, "Would you like some help?" I released her and saw the answer to my question in her eyes.

Keeping my voice loud, I said to her, "Elaine, I know I've got a nerve, but could you drive me over to my mum's? My car's just broken down, and there isn't a direct bus which can take me there. Mum's not well as you know."

Her date turned to me and gave me a dismissive look. He said, "Elaine is on a date. With me."

I said to him, "This is urgent. Very urgent. My mum was expecting me an hour ago."

"Then get a taxi," he snapped. "Elaine and I have a lot to discuss. We have holiday plans to talk about."

I faced Elaine and said, "I didn't realise I was interrupting. Don't worry about me. I can get a taxi. I hope it doesn't take too long. Mum will be so worried."

"There's no need to phone for a taxi," Elaine said. "I will drive you there immediately."

The man said to Elaine, "You can't leave me. I haven't finished talking to you yet. Tell this woman to clear off and get a taxi."

Elaine let out a gasp of outrage. "What a selfish thing to say! Kevin, you are not the kind of man I'm looking for. Goodbye!" She put her hand on my arm and led me out of the pub. Kevin muttered something, but we ignored him.

As soon as we got outside, Elaine started laughing. She said, "I couldn't get rid of him! He wouldn't stop talking. I couldn't get a word in. Thanks for your help."

"That's okay." I noticed Peggy waiting a bit further up the road. She was sending quizzical looks our way.

Elaine said, "I'll be off now before Kevin comes out. Thanks again. Perhaps we'll bump into each other again soon."

"Perhaps we will," I replied.

Elaine said goodbye and walked away. As soon as she'd gone, Peggy came over to me.

I said to Peggy, "I like Elaine. I hope we can do something to stop my vision coming true. I don't like the idea of some strange man hurting her."

Peggy gave my arm a reassuring pat. "We'll do all that we can."

# Chapter 13

Two completed jumpers were waiting for us at the café.

Erin met us at the door with a huge smile on her face. She said, "You should hear how much Celia has been bossing Robbie around! She's been getting him to do all sorts of things for her. And my kind-hearted husband has agreed to everything she's asked for. I feel so sorry for him. But it is fun to watch."

"He's too kind-hearted by half," Peggy said. "Where is he?"

"Over here," Erin said.

We followed her over to the area where the sofas were. Peggy and I stopped in our tracks when we saw what Robbie was doing to Celia.

Celia was leaning back on one of the sofas with her arms stretched out in front of her. Robbie was kneeling at her feet and caressing her hands.

I hissed to Erin, "What's he doing?"

She hissed back, "Giving her a hand massage. She said her fingers were hurting from all that knitting. He couldn't say no to her."

"He could," Peggy said. "Let's put an end to this nonsense right now." She marched over to Celia and stood in front of her. "What's going on?"

Celia jumped at Peggy's stern expression. "This young man is massaging my aching fingers if you must know. He's doing a wonderful job."

Peggy pointed an accusing finger at Celia. "In all the years I've known you, you've never had aching fingers. You are taking advantage of Robbie, and you know it."

"He doesn't mind," Celia replied defensively.

Robbie said, "Well, I do have other things to—"

Celia interrupted him, "You've got a lovely touch, Robbie. You didn't mind giving me a back massage earlier on, did you? No, you didn't. And you don't mind giving my hands a massage now, do you?"

Robbie tried again, "Well, I—"

"No, you don't," Celia spoke for him. "You can give me a head massage next. You've got a magical touch. Keep going. I feel all warm and tingly."

Peggy exploded, "Celia! I did not ask you to come here so you could feel all warm and tingly! Behave yourself. Robbie, release her hands."

Robbie dropped Celia's hands and stood up.

Peggy stared at Celia. Celia stared back at her. There was a tense atmosphere in the room and it felt like everyone was holding their breaths.

Peggy and Celia suddenly burst into laughter.

Celia said, "Sorry, Peg. I couldn't resist the chance to have a young man's hands on me! It's been decades."

"I should have known better than to have put temptation in your way," Peggy said with a chuckle.

Robbie's head dropped and he muttered, "I feel used."

Erin went over to him and put her arm around his waist. "You should feel flattered. This just proves how irresistible you are to women. It's not just me who can see how wonderful you are."

He lifted his head. "I still feel used."

"Can I do something to make you feel better?" Erin asked with a small grin.

Robbie brightened up.

Before he could speak, I said, "Can we stop with all this talk about touching and feeling warm and tingly? It's making me feel very uncomfortable."

Peggy said, "Karis is right. This is a place for business, not a den of iniquity. Robbie, Erin, if you're going to get all mushy with each other, do it elsewhere. Celia, clear all thoughts of being warm and tingly from your mind and tell me where the completed jumpers are."

"They're right behind you on that table," Celia said.

I looked that way and noticed Celia's friends sitting on the opposite sofa. They were engrossed in their knitting and didn't look our way.

Celia continued, "We've only made a couple, but we'll have another one done soon."

"A couple might be enough," I said. I made a move towards them and then stopped. I cast a cautious glance at Celia.

Peggy picked up on what I was thinking and said to me, "It's okay. Celia knows about your psychic abilities." She looked at Celia. "This is why I wanted you to knit these jumpers. Karis is getting funny feelings about the knitting patterns."

Celia's eyes widened. "How exciting. I've never seen anyone being psychic before. Go on, Karis, pick the jumpers up and have a good feel. Get your psychic powers revved up."

Celia's friends stopped knitting and watched me as I picked up a jumper. I could feel all eyes on me now. I pulled the jumper closer and closed my eyes.

Nothing.

I put that jumper down and tried the other.

Still nothing.

I shook my head. "I'm not getting anything. Perhaps it should have been me who knitted them like I did with the twin set."

Peggy said, "Perhaps. Don't forget that you got a strong vision when you wore the twin set. I know that jumper is too big for you, but put it on anyway."

I did so. The jumper was huge on me and the sleeves dangled over my hands. I took some deep breaths. I was fully aware of being watched and I felt immense pressure to perform.

No visions came to me.

Peggy clicked her fingers. "I know what you have to do! Get a man to wear the jumpers. That might cause something to happen. Robbie, you'll do."

Robbie removed himself from Erin's embrace and said, "I am a person with feelings, you know. I don't appreciate being treated as an object." He came over to me and held his hand out. "Give me the jumper, Karis. Let's get this over with." Despite his act of martyrdom, I saw the sparkle of glee in his eyes.

I handed the jumper over and said, "You're enjoying every minute of this."

He smiled but didn't say anything as he took the jumper.

Celia said, "Hang on a minute. That jumper won't fit you, Robbie. I've been sizing you up and that one is far too small for you. The other one is too. Are there any other men around?" She looked around the café as if expecting a group of men to pop out from behind the tables.

My good friend, Seb Parker, chose that moment to come into the café. The smile on his face froze when he saw many pairs of interested eyes looking his way.

Celia stood up, faced Seb and said, "You'll do. Get over here. We need your body."

Seb didn't move. He looked at me and said, "Karis?" His eyes went to Robbie. "Robbie?"

Robbie cried out jovially, "Run for your life, Seb! It's too late for me, but you can save yourself! Run!"

Peggy dashed over to Seb at an amazing speed. She grabbed his arm and dragged him over to the sofas. He looked frightened to death.

Seb muttered, "I only came in to talk to Karis. I wish I'd phoned her now." He gave me a beseeching look. "What's going on?"

He jumped when he felt Celia's hands on him. She looked him up and down and proclaimed, "You'll do nicely. You're a perfect specimen. Yes, quite perfect. Do you work out? You must do. Flex your muscles. Have you got a six-pack? Lift your shirt and let's have a look."

"Celia!" Peggy snapped. "Back in your cage. Seb, sorry about Celia. Would you mind trying some jumpers on, please?"

"Why?" He took a step away from Celia who was still sizing him up.

I quickly explained about the other knitting patterns and how the completed jumpers might help me.

Seb smiled at me. "In that case, of course I'll try them on." He took his jacket off and pulled one of the jumpers over his head. He held his arms out and said, "What happens next? Do you need to touch me?"

Heat rushed to my cheeks and I looked away. I mumbled, "I think so."

Celia said, "Go on then, Karis. Get on with it. Have a good feel. We're all watching."

I looked at her and said, "I know. That's the problem. I need some privacy. I can't perform with an audience."

"Try," Celia said.

Robbie came to my rescue. "Celia, there's been enough touching in this café today. Karis needs some privacy, and that's what she's going to get. Haven't you got some knitting to do?"

"Party pooper," Celia muttered as she returned to the sofa.

"Karis," Robbie went on, "take Seb upstairs. The building work has been completed up there. Take your time. I know this is important. I won't let anyone disturb you. Seb, there's another jumper to try on too."

I gave him a grateful smile and then headed for the stairs. Seb took the other jumper and followed me.

Once upstairs, Seb smiled kindly and said, "Well, what do we do now?" He opened his arms wide. "Would you like a hug? You look as if you could use one." He waggled his eyebrows at me. "Come on, Karis, you know you want to."

I laughed. "I'm only hugging you because of my visions."

"Keep telling yourself that," Seb joked.

I moved closer to Seb and he put his arms around me. I rested my chin on his shoulder. The jumper felt soft under me. Seb's arms were warm.

The area around me began to fade, and a buzzing noise settled in my ears.

I prepared myself for a vision.

# Chapter 14

The vision came and went in a few seconds. I stepped out of Seb's embrace and tried to make sense of what had just happened.

Seb said, "Did you see something?"

"No, but I felt something. I took on that woman's memories again as I hugged you. She must have had her eyes closed because I couldn't see anything. But I could sense her feelings. You're not the right man."

"Pardon? But you told me to put the jumper on."

"I don't mean it in that way. The woman was thinking this about the man she was with. He's not the right one. He's second-best. She felt sad about it but resigned to the fact. It was a hopeless cause, but one she had to put up with. I didn't love you. You'll never be the right one for me. Her, I mean."

Seb's lips pressed together, and I saw hurt in his eyes.

"Seb, you do know I'm not talking about you and me, don't you? I'm speaking from the perspective of the woman in my vision."

He smiled tightly. "I know. Shall I try the other jumper on?"

"Might as well. Thank you."

"It's okay. What are friends for?"

He quickly changed jumpers and we hugged again. Seb's hug didn't feel as warm this time. It was clear I'd upset him. I pushed that thought out of my mind and concentrated on my vision.

Another vision swiftly came to me, and just as quickly, it fled.

Seb whipped his arms away. "Well?" he asked. "Am I still second-best?"

"Seb," I began warily, "this isn't about you. But yes, the feelings were just the same."

There was a polite cough behind us. Peggy stood there with her eyes closed and her hand held out. She said, "I don't want to interrupt, but the next jumper is ready. Here."

"You can open your eyes," I said to her. I walked over and took the completed jumper.

Peggy opened her eyes. "Any news?" she asked. She stole a glance at Seb. "What's wrong with him? Why's he sulking?"

"I'll explain later. Thanks for this."

Peggy took another look at Seb before walking down the stairs.

I gave the jumper to Seb. He did have a sulky look on his face. I smiled and said, "Stop being such a twit. You know those feelings have nothing to do with us and our friendship."

He shrugged. "So, you don't feel that I'm second-best then?"

I moved my hand in a rocking motion. "You're okay. I can take you or leave you."

Seb broke into a laugh. "I deserved that. Sorry for being a twit. It's just that, you know, things have happened in the past to me which have made me feel second-best."

"Things have happened to all of us," I said kindly. "Put that jumper on, open your arms and wrap them around me. You're the one who needs a hug now."

Seb pulled the jumper on and we embraced again.

The vision that came to me was different now. I saw a man's face in front of me. He looked middle-aged. It wasn't the young man who I'd seen at the cinema.

The man smiled warmly at me, ran a hand down his jumper and said, "Thank you for making this new one for me. It's lovely. It'll keep me warm and snug on those cold days when I'm outside. I'll think of you when I'm wearing it."

I felt my heart fill with love at the tender look in his eyes. He really was a kind, thoughtful man. I was lucky to have him in my life. I moved forward and put my arms around him. My head rested on his chest. I felt safe and secure. Nothing could hurt me when he was around.

The vision faded, but I didn't move. I stayed right where I was and experienced the afterglow of those loving feelings. It was like being woken from a wonderful dream and I had to hang on to those lovely feelings as long as possible.

I let out a sigh of contentment.

Seb said, "Karis? Have you come back to me?"

"Shh," I mumbled. I rested my head on his chest. I could hear Seb's heart beating. I knew full well it was Seb I was hugging now. He was nice to hug. So solid and dependable.

"Karis?"

"Quiet. I'm revelling in the wake of joy and love."

Seb moved me to arm's-length and looked down at me. His eyes widened as he took in my expression. He said softly, "Karis, what happened? You're glowing. Your eyes are," he swallowed, "full of love."

"I'm not surprised." I took a step back. I explained what I'd experienced.

Seb nodded. "So, the woman in the vision now loves this man?"

"Very much so. He's not the man who was at the cinema with her. But that particular man comes into her life in later years and threatens her." I shook my head. "I can't make sense of it."

Seb considered the matter. "This woman was originally stood up by that young man at the cinema. Perhaps she ended up marrying someone else whom she considered second-best. But over the years, she learned to love him. She must have felt some affection for him if she kept knitting jumpers for him."

"That's true. But why does the original man come back and accuse her of murder? And why does he attack her?"

"That is a mystery. Do you know where the knitting patterns came from yet?"

Like a genie in a bottle, Peggy suddenly appeared at the top of the steps. She announced, "We have a suspect!"

"How long have you been standing there?" Seb asked. "Have you been listening to everything we said? Have you been watching our every move?"

Peggy retorted, "That's neither here nor there, Seb Parker. The point is, we have a suspect. Her name is Elaine and we know where she lives. She's meeting an old flame tonight in a restaurant. He could be the mystery man who attacks her."

"How do you know all of this?" Seb asked. "On second thoughts, I don't want to know."

Peggy continued, "We don't know which restaurant she's going to meet this man in. But we need to know what he looks like. Can you find out? Can you drive past her house and aim a listening machine at it? Something that will pick up her conversations? We could find out what time they're meeting and where."

"No," Seb replied.

"How about tapping into her phone and her messages?" Peggy persisted.

"No."

"What about running a police check on her and finding out if she's got any skeletons in the wardrobe. Or hidden in her cellar?"

"Peggy, I'm not going to do any of that." Seb looked at me. "Do you think Elaine is in danger?"

"She could be," I said. "But I'm not sure. I'd need to see what this old boyfriend of hers looks like."

Seb nodded. "And she's going to meet him tonight?"

"She is," I confirmed.

Peggy tutted. "I just told you that."

Seb ignored her. "In that case, I could keep a surveillance of her house and see when she leaves. I could let you know the name of the restaurant she goes to, and then you can have a look at her companion."

"That would really help," I said. "Thank you."

"What are friends for?" he said. He looked at me for slightly too long. "Once I know the name of the restaurant, I'll pick you up and we'll have a look at this old boyfriend together."

Peggy prodded him. "What about me? I want to look at him too."

Seb gave Peggy a patient smile. "I'll pick you up too. I'll be in touch later." He pulled the jumper off and gave it to me. "If anything happens in the meantime, get in touch with me. Don't put yourself in danger."

"We won't," Peggy said.

Seb shared a smile with me before walking away.

Peggy said, "What's going on with you and Seb?"

"Nothing. We're just friends."

"Really? Friends don't look at each other like that. You watch yourself around Seb. You've only just got a divorce. You don't want to get involved with another man yet."

"He's just a friend," I insisted.

Peggy gave me a look but didn't say anything.

I went on, "He's a very helpful friend. Thanks to him, we'll be able to go to this restaurant tonight and look at that old boyfriend of Elaine's. We'll stop any murders taking place."

"I suppose Seb does have his uses," Peggy relented. Her eyes narrowed. "Why do you look so worried?"

"I don't know. I've had a niggling feeling for the last few hours, and I can't work out what's wrong." I gave her a small smile. "It'll come to me."

# Chapter 15

Peggy and I went downstairs. We were met by the curious looks of Celia and her knitting friends as they stared at us from the sofas.

"Well?" Celia asked. "What happened? Did you see something? Smell something? How does it work? Can you tell fortunes? Do you know the lottery numbers for next week?"

Peggy said, "Stop badgering her, Celia. It takes a lot out of Karis when she has these visions. Some of them can be quite upsetting."

I said to Peggy, "I don't mind talking about my visions. It might help to make sense of them if I talk about what I saw."

Celia shuffled along the sofa and patted the empty space at her side. "Sit next to me. Tell me everything."

I settled myself next to Celia and explained what I'd witnessed. I also told her what Seb's opinion of the situation was. Her friends paused in their knitting and listened attentively.

At some point, Robbie appeared with a cup of coffee for me and slid it onto the table before quickly moving away. I think he was nervous about being so close to Celia.

Once I'd told Celia and her friends about my recent visions, I filled them in on my previous ones.

When I'd finished, Celia concluded, "I agree with your handsome friend, Seb. It sounds like our mystery knitter didn't want to be with the man she was knitting for, at first. But as the years went on, she fell in love with him. I'm intrigued by this young man in the cinema.

Why does he come back to attack the mystery knitter in the present day?"

I said, "I don't know the answer to that. And I'm not entirely convinced our mystery knitter is Elaine, but Peggy and I are going to check on her companion tonight at the restaurant." I paused and looked at the knitting patterns on the table. "I keep thinking I'm missing something, though." I looked over at Peggy who was perched on the end of the sofa. "I think we should go to that charity shop where Jade possibly bought the patterns. There could be something important there. Perhaps there will be other belongings which came with the patterns."

Peggy nodded. "Good thinking. We'll do that now."

"Peg, do you still want us to carry on with these jumpers?" Celia asked. "We've done five now. I don't mind staying here and carrying on. I like it here. And I like the company." She cast a glance at Robbie who had just come out of the kitchen. He saw Celia grinning at him, spun around and scuttled back into the kitchen.

Peggy raised her eyebrows in my direction. "What do you think? Do you still need the jumpers?"

I picked the nearest pattern up. A flash of a man's face came into my mind. The image vanished quickly and I couldn't work out who he was. I said to Celia, "Yes, it would really help me if you could finish these. If you don't mind?"

"I don't mind at all," Celia confirmed. "You and Peg get yourselves off to the charity shop. Leave the patterns to us. Let us know how you get on." She picked her knitting needles up and added, "If this week's lottery numbers come to you while you're out and about, let me know what they are."

I quickly drank the coffee before heading to the kitchen. I told Erin and Robbie about my latest visions and advised them where I was going next.

Robbie cast a wary look towards the café area. He said, "How long do you think Celia will be here?"

Erin patted his arm. "Don't you worry about Celia and her roving hands. I'll be the one who takes food and drinks out to our guests."

She looked my way. "Take care, Karis. Even though you're not saying it, I can tell how worried you are."

I was going to say I wasn't worried at all, but there was no point lying to Erin. She knew me too well.

Peggy and I headed over to the charity shop.

As we went through the door, Peggy said, "Ah, the manager is in today. It's Irene. I used to work with her a while back. She's a good sort, but she can talk till the cows come home. Let me talk to her first."

"I will do." I was happy to do that as my mind was already elsewhere. As soon as we'd entered the shop, my scalp had begun to prickle with apprehension. There was something important in here. I scanned the packed shelves and my heart sank. There were hundreds of items in here. How was I going to narrow down what the important object was?

I followed Peggy over to the counter. A woman a bit younger than Peggy was standing behind it. She was wearing many colours in a variety of styles. Three beaded necklaces around her neck clicked together as she sorted out a tray of bracelets in front of her. As Peggy and I approached, she looked up and broke into a smile.

"Hello, Irene," Peggy said.

"Peggy! How are you? I haven't seen you for a few months. Are you still doing volunteer work at the hospital? I keep meaning to pop down there and do some myself, but you know me and hospitals. I'm worried that if I go in, I won't come out again." She laughed loudly and her necklaces jangled together.

"I do still volunteer," Peggy said. "Irene, we're here about—"

"I heard you were doing stuff online," Irene interrupted her. "I don't know how you do it. I can't make head nor tails of that world web thing. Our Steve keeps telling me it's easy, but it's not easy for me. I tried to order a book online the other day. I ended up getting a pair of walking boots delivered. I don't know how that happened."

"Irene," Peggy tried again.

"And you've been doing classes at Erin's Café, so I've heard. How you find the time and energy, I don't know. I can barely find the energy to come here every day. You know what I'm like with my troubles, Peggy. I've been to the doctors this morning about them, and he's put me on different medication. I hope it does the trick."

Peggy's voice was a tad louder this time as she said, "Irene, we want to talk to you about some knitting patterns we've got. They might have come from this shop. I've got one in my bag." She reached into her bag and pulled out the twin set pattern. She gave it to Irene.

Irene looked at it and then lowered it. "You'd be amazed at the things we get in here. A surprising number of false legs, for some reason. Do people keep spares and then no longer need them? We get false teeth too. Would you believe it! False teeth."

"The knitting pattern?" Peggy said with a hint of annoyance in her voice. "Does it look familiar?"

Irene put her attention back on the pattern. "Oh, yes. I remember this. A bunch of patterns came in a few weeks ago. I didn't think anyone would want them with the styles being so old-fashioned. But one of our regulars bought them. A young woman who always wears black. I thought she was going to a funeral when I first met her months ago, but no, she just likes to wear black for some reason. Aren't people strange? There was a man last week who—"

I thought I saw steam coming from Peggy's ears, so I swiftly interrupted Irene and said, "Sorry to be brusque, but we're in a rush. Do you know who donated the patterns?"

"Yes," Irene replied.

"And who was it?" Peggy asked.

"It was a woman. I would guess she was in her early fifties. Maybe late fifties. It's hard to tell these days with all that age-defying cream that everyone buys. She brought a whole stack of stuff in. She said they belonged to her dad who passed away a while back. Her mum refused to get rid of his belongings and they'd been cluttering up the house. But the daughter had insisted on getting rid of her dad's stuff and brought them here." She gave the pattern back to Peggy. "This was definitely with the items she brought in."

Peggy leaned closer to Irene and said, "Where are those belongings now?"

"I've sold them all. They went really quickly."

"You sold all of them?" There was disappointment in Peggy's voice.

I asked, "What items did that woman bring in? Besides the knitting patterns."

Irene replied, "There were some men's shoes and slippers, and some trousers and jackets. Oh, and some knitted jumpers too. They were in good condition and I sold them in a day."

Peggy's shoulders dropped. "I don't suppose you know the name of the woman who brought the items in?"

Irene shook her head. "I don't. She was in a rush. All the belongings were in a suitcase and she just left it next to this counter."

My heart missed a beat. "A suitcase? Do you still have it?"

Irene frowned. "I do. Tatty old thing, it is. I can't sell it, not in that condition."

"Where is it now?" I asked, half-fearing the answer.

"It's in the back. I was going to take it to the tip later."

"Can I have a look at it? Please?" I heard the pleading tone in my voice, but I couldn't help it.

Irene's eyes narrowed. "Why would you want to look at it? It's a scruffy-looking thing. It's no good to anyone."

Peggy said, "People say that about me, but I'm still useful. We'll pay you for it, Irene."

Irene shook her head at us and then walked away from the counter.

Peggy said to me, "Is the suitcase important?"

I nodded. "I had a funny feeling about something the minute we came in here. When Irene mentioned the suitcase, I knew it must be that."

Irene returned with an old-fashioned suitcase. It was of a medium size and was brown in colour. The bottom edges were scuffed, and there were a couple of tears in the top corner. I already had a ten-pound-note ready and I handed it to Irene.

Irene swapped the suitcase for the money and said, "This is too much money. Let me get you some change."

"No, keep it all," I said. I was eager to get out of the shop and to have some alone time with the suitcase.

"If you're sure? Thank you." Irene moved over to the till and opened it. With her eyes on the till, she said, "Peggy, I haven't told you about our Steve and his latest divorce. You won't believe what's happened now."

Peggy grabbed my arm and announced, "No time to talk, Irene! Bye for now." She propelled me out of the charity shop and on to the path outside in record time.

Once we were a safe distance from the shop, we looked at the tatty suitcase in my hand.

Peggy gave me an expectant look. "Well?"

# Chapter 16

"Well?" Seb asked me later that evening. We were sitting in his car outside a restaurant. "Was there something inside the suitcase? Some valuable clue hidden inside the lining?"

"No," I replied.

He continued, "Did you get a vision? A feeling?"

"No." I paused and tried to find the right words. "But something will come to me soon about it. That suitcase is important for some reason. Do you know that feeling you get when something is on its way to you? Like a parcel or something? You have this feeling of anticipation. You know it will arrive, but you don't know when."

Seb nodded.

I put my hands on my stomach. "This is what I'm feeling now. I can't rush the vision, but I know it's going to arrive at some point."

Peggy popped her head forward from the back seat. "I had to wait in all day once for a new fridge. They said it would be there between eight a.m. and six p.m., but they couldn't give me a specific time. I was on tenterhooks all day as I waited for that fridge. I didn't even go to the toilet in case I missed the delivery." She sighed at the memory. "That was not a good day. Seb, are you sure this is the right restaurant? Did you see Elaine go inside?"

"For the third time, yes." Seb turned in his seat so he could look at Peggy better. "Are you sure you don't want to sit in the front? You'll get a better view of the restaurant from here. I don't mind sitting in the back while we wait."

"No, thanks. I've got my knitting things on the back seat now. And my snacks." She frowned at the building in front of us. "You can't see a thing through those frosted windows. Are you sure she's in there?"

Seb pointed to a red car parked a short distance away. "That's her car. She's still inside."

"What about her date?" Peggy persisted. "Has he arrived? Where is he now?"

Seb said, "I don't know the answer to either question. As soon as Elaine came here, I drove away and collected you and Karis."

Peggy gave him a sniff of disapproval. "Some police stakeout this is. You're not even doing it right."

Keeping his tone patient, Seb explained, "This isn't a stakeout. This isn't official police business. I'm doing this for a friend." He smiled at me.

Peggy coughed.

Seb corrected himself, "I'm doing this for two dear friends."

"But we need to see Elaine's date," Peggy argued. "We can't sit here for hours on the off chance that we get a look at him. Go inside, Seb. Have a good nosy. Can't you use your police powers or something?"

"As I've just explained, this isn't a police matter. However, there is something I can do." He put his hand on the door handle. "I'm going inside. Peggy, do not follow me. Is that clear?"

She looked away from his glance. "What if I need to use the ladies?"

"You've just been," Seb pointed out. "I made sure of that before we left. I'm leaving the car now. Do not follow me." He gave Peggy another look before exiting the car.

Peggy chuckled as we watched Seb walking towards the restaurant. She said, "He's a bossy one, isn't he? I've a good mind to follow him just to annoy him. But I won't. I know he's doing us a big favour with this stakeout business."

"He is," I said. "I hope he doesn't get into trouble because of it."

"Me too. I'd better get back to my knitting. I've already completed the back of the last jumper. We'll have ten completed jumpers soon. It was good of Celia and her gang to do those other jumpers for us.

I'll send them a thank-you gift." She shuffled back on her seat and I soon heard the clicking of knitting needles.

I said, "I'll send them something too." I kept my eyes on Seb as he entered the restaurant. He came back out a few minutes later and got back into the car.

He handed his phone to me and said, "Look at the photo. It's the man who's sitting with Elaine. This is the best I could do while being discreet. Does he look familiar?"

I squinted at the image and then enlarged it. "It's hard to say. I can only see half of his face. He looks to be of the right age. Did you get any other photos of him?"

"No. Sorry." Seb took his phone back.

From the back seat, Peggy said, "How did you take that secret photo without him seeing you?"

Seb replied loftily, "I am a highly trained officer of the law who has specialized knowledge in the art of covert surveillance. I can't reveal my methods to a member of the public."

A snort came from the back seat followed by the clicking of needles. Peggy said, "Did you go to the toilet and then sneak a photo on the way back out? That's what I would have done."

Seb's mouth twitched. "Perhaps I did. Perhaps I didn't."

I said to him, "Did you get a good look at his face? The man in my vision had brown eyes."

He shook his head. "He was sitting opposite Elaine and had his back to me. Elaine seemed happy in his company. They were chatting a lot and smiling. She doesn't look as if she's in any danger."

"Yet," Peggy added darkly from behind us.

A funny noise came from Seb. He grimaced. "Sorry. That's my stomach rumbling. I haven't had anything to eat for hours. And the food inside the restaurant smells delicious."

We both jumped as something appeared between our seats.

"Pork pie?" Peggy waggled the item in Seb's direction. "I've got sausage rolls and sandwiches too. I've also got a flask of tea. I thought we might be here a while."

Seb took the pork pie and ate it with relish. He then accepted two sausage rolls, a ham sandwich and a packet of crisps. I was too nervous to eat, so I only had a cup of tea.

I'd just finished the drink when the door to the restaurant opened and Elaine came out.

Peggy declared, "Battle stations! Eyes at the ready, Karis. Seb, switch the engine on. Be prepared to tail the suspect."

Seb said, "We won't be tailing anyone, Peggy." But he reached for his keys anyway.

I looked closer at the man who was talking to Elaine. I said, "It's not him."

Peggy said, "Are you sure? Take another look."

"I'm certain. His face is the wrong shape. And his hair is different at the front. It's not the man I saw in my vision." I pressed my lips together. I didn't know whether to be pleased or not.

Seb put his hand on my arm and said softly, "Don't sound so disappointed. At least we know Elaine isn't in any danger now."

"But who is in danger?" I said. "I'm missing something obvious, and I don't know what it is."

"What can I do to help?" Seb asked.

Hopelessness washed over me. "I don't know." Tears came to my eyes. "I have to do something, but I don't know what. Why am I getting these visions if they don't make any sense?"

Peggy put a comforting hand on my shoulder. "It'll come to you, Karis. Don't force it. I'll finish this jumper by tomorrow and then we'll see if it's of any use."

Seb added, "I'm sure you'll pick up on something else soon."

"I hope you're right." I looked out of the window and saw Elaine embracing her date. She waved goodbye to him and then got into her car. Her date watched her drive away before he left.

# Chapter 17

I couldn't sleep at all that night. Every time I closed my eyes, all my previous visions flashed into my mind. It was like a film stuck in a continuous loop. Why were they in my mind? What was I missing?

I gave up on sleep in the early hours and got up. I made myself a cup of tea and then decided to write down my visions. Perhaps writing the details down would trigger something in my brain.

It didn't. I was none the wiser.

I thought back to the incidents which had led to my visions, starting from the knitting event at the café. I wrote as much as I could remember. The sun was coming up by now and I quickly made myself another tea.

As I wrote about visiting the three knitters in their homes, I got a buzzing sound in my ears. Something was coming to me. I continued writing and put as much information as I could remember about each woman we'd been to see. They had all mentioned a daughter. Irene at the charity shop had told us someone's daughter had brought the knitting patterns in. So, the daughter aspect didn't help me. I closed my eyes and tried to recall every tiny detail of our visits to those homes and what had been said.

Then it hit me.

The thing which had been niggling me.

That image which I'd discounted as not being important.

I remembered it clearly now.

When Peggy and I had driven away from the last woman's house, Martha, I'd spotted a car parked on the opposite side of the road. The driver's window had been down, and I'd got a look at the man inside as he stared in the direction of Martha's house. He was wearing sunglasses, but the jut of his chin was familiar.

It was the older man from my vision. I knew that for certain now. The woman who he was going to attack was Martha. Or had he already attacked her?

I jumped to my feet, grabbed my handbag and raced for the door. I rushed around to Peggy's house but stopped when I noticed her bedroom curtains were closed. She always opened them within minutes of getting up. I checked my watch. It was only seven a.m. Peggy could have been up most of the night knitting that last jumper. I didn't want to disturb her sleep. I left a text message for her and then got into my car.

Before I set off, I phoned Seb. He didn't answer, so I left him a message and gave him Martha's address. I told him I'd meet him there.

My heart was pounding in my chest and I had to wipe my sweaty palms on my jeans as I drove along. Was I going to be too late? Had the incident already occurred? Had Martha attacked that man in self-defence? Was he dead?

When I reached Martha's house, I spotted the car which had been parked there previously. It was empty. Where was the driver? I knew I wouldn't be able to wait for Seb. I had to make sure Martha was okay.

I jumped out of my car and ran down the driveway. I came to a sudden stop when I saw the back door was ajar. I could hear raised voices coming from inside.

Martha's pleading tone came to me, "I don't know what you're talking about. I haven't seen him in years."

A man's voice replied, "Stop lying to me! I know you killed him."

I pushed the door open and went inside. I followed the sound of the voices to the living room.

Just like my vision, the man was inches away from Martha. Fury twisted his features. His hands were moving towards Martha's neck. She looked petrified. I saw her hand scrambling for something at her side. There was a knitting bag next to her chair which hadn't been there yesterday. Martha's hand alighted on a knitting needle.

"No!" I screamed. I moved forward and grabbed the man by his shoulders. I yanked him backwards and we fell onto the carpet together.

He roared with rage and tried to get to his feet. He hissed at me, "She killed my brother! She won't get away with it!"

A shadow covered his face as Martha loomed behind him. She plunged a knitting needle into his neck.

The man's mouth opened in shock. His eyes fluttered and then closed. He slithered to the floor.

Martha screamed and dropped the needle. Her hands flew to her face.

Blood gushed from the man's neck at an impossibly fast rate. I put my hands over the wound and called out, "Phone an ambulance! Quick!"

Martha lowered her hands and mumbled, "I didn't mean to do it. I didn't."

"An ambulance! Now!" I ordered. My hands weren't doing a good job of stemming the flow of blood. I could almost feel the life slipping away from the man.

I shouted at Martha again, and she finally moved. I looked down at the pale man and said, "Don't die. Hold on."

# Chapter 18

I was still shaking thirty minutes later. I was at the hospital and sitting on a plastic chair in a corridor. Despite washing my hands many times, I could still see blood under my nails. My sleeves were covered in it.

Seb came over to me and handed me a hot drink. He sat down and said, "How are you doing?"

I lifted the cup and took a small sip. The tea was weak but at least it was hot. "I'm fine. I think. How's Martha?"

"She's okay. She's being treated for shock. She hasn't suffered any physical injuries."

I took another drink of the tea. "What about that man? Is he okay? He lost a lot of blood." I tried to smile. "Most of it is on me."

"His name is Morgan Booker, and he's okay. He did lose a lot of blood, but he'll survive, thanks to you."

"Have you spoken to him yet? Have you found out why he was at Martha's house?"

"Not yet. He keeps drifting in and out of sleep. I'll speak to him soon. He's not going anywhere."

I hesitated before asking my next question. "What about this brother of his? Have you found out anything about him? He said Martha murdered him."

Seb gave me a slow nod. "I've made some enquiries. He did have a younger brother called Finley who went missing years ago. Karis, he went missing in 1958."

My hands shook. Seb swiftly took the cup from my hands before I spilled tea all over myself. "1958?" I repeated.

Seb put the cup on a table at his side. "Yes. I've made a few checks and discovered Finley Booker was registered as a missing person by his brother in that year." He took a deep breath before continuing, "Finley was last seen heading for the cinema in town. He was going on a date."

"With Martha?"

He nodded. "With Martha. He never turned up. He didn't return home, and his family became concerned. His brother never gave up looking for him, according to the police reports."

"Did the police question Martha about Finley's disappearance?"

"They did. I've managed to have a look at her statement. She claimed she'd been dating Finley for a few months, and it was serious between them. She was due to meet him that night outside the cinema, but he never showed up. He never contacted her again." He reached into his pocket. "I've got a picture of Finley Booker. It was in Morgan's wallet. Do you feel up to looking at it?"

I nodded and held my palm out. Seb put the small black and white photo in my hand. I looked at the smiling young man. I said, "It's him. It's the man I saw inside the cinema."

We were silent for a while.

I spoke first. "Does this mean Martha killed Finley?"

"I don't know yet," Seb answered quietly. "Once the doctor has finished with her, I'll take her down to the station and question her there. I wish you could sit in on the interview, but that isn't possible."

I shook my head in disbelief. "I can't believe Martha is a killer. Why would she kill Finley if she loved him so much?"

"We don't know that she did yet. But I do know she lied to you."

"About what?"

"About the twin set," Seb explained. "You told me she'd denied knitting it when Peggy showed her the pattern."

"She did. She said the pattern was too complicated for her. How do you know she lied to me?"

"It was in the police report she gave in 1958," Seb said. "She went into great detail about how excited she was for her date with

Finley Booker. She explained how she'd knitted a special twin set in a light blue colour. It was going to be a surprise for Finley. She even mentioned the film which had inspired her to make it. It was the film we saw together in Charles' cinema."

My shoulders dropped. "I can't believe she lied. She seemed so sincere."

"Killers often do." He squeezed my hand. "You saved Morgan's life. If you hadn't been there, he would have bled to death. I'm going to drive you home now. Try and get some sleep. Although, I'm not sure that'll be possible with that nosy neighbour of yours. Peggy's already left me ten messages about your whereabouts."

"She's probably left some for me too. I haven't checked my phone for a while." Weariness settled on my shoulders like a heavy blanket. "Why would Martha kill him? She loved him."

Seb pulled me to my feet. "Don't you worry about that. I'll speak to Martha later and get to the bottom of this."

"Will you let me know what she says? Are you allowed to do that?"

"It depends what she says. I'll phone you later after I've spoken to her. Come on; let's get you home."

# Chapter 19

Peggy was waiting for me in my living room. She gasped when I walked in and cried out, "Is that blood on you? Is it yours? Who's dead?"

"Nobody, thank goodness." I walked over to the sofa and was about to collapse into it, but Peggy grabbed my arm and said, "Don't sit down, you'll get blood everywhere. It's a nuisance to get out."

"It's dry. Mainly," I looked at the stains on my clothes and grimaced. "I didn't realise there was so much of it."

Peggy pulled me towards the door. "Go and have a shower. Leave these clothes outside the bathroom, and I'll deal with them."

"But don't you want to know what happened? Don't you want to know whose blood this is?"

"As long as it's not yours, that's all I care about. I'm presuming from your earlier message that Martha is our mystery knitter. You can tell me everything once you're clean. I can't listen to you while you look like something from a horror movie." She pushed me towards the stairs.

I had a shower and changed into fresh clothes. I went downstairs and found Peggy sitting at the kitchen table. Two cups of tea were on the table along with a plate of toast.

Peggy pushed the plate towards me and said, "Eat something."

"I don't know if I can." I sat down and picked up the cup.

"You can, and you will," Peggy said. "And once you've told me what's been going on, you can take yourself off to bed and get some sleep. Did you manage any sleep last night?"

I shook my head and then had a quick drink of tea. It was much better than the hospital one. Under Peggy's watchful eye, I had a slice of toast. After I'd eaten it, I told her about Martha and her visit from Morgan Booker. Peggy's eyes widened when I got to the part about Seb meeting me at the hospital and what Seb had told me.

Peggy shook her head in disbelief. "Martha lied to us. I feel so betrayed. I connected with her over our late husbands. She lied about being a knitter too. All that nonsense about not being able to knit because of her arthritis. She took us for fools. When she stabbed Morgan in the neck, did she have a manic look in her eyes? Did she look as if she was enjoying it? As if she'd done it before?"

"I don't know. It all happened so quickly. She seemed remorseful afterwards and covered her face with her hands."

Peggy said sagely, "Probably to cover the glee on her face. I wonder how she killed Finley? And where his body is now. I suppose Seb will let us know in due course. Have another slice of toast."

I dutifully did as I was told.

Peggy leaned back in her chair and said, "I finished that other jumper this morning. It's in your living room. I don't suppose you need it now. I can take it to the charity shop later. I'll take those that Celia made too. I hope Irene doesn't go on too much when I pop in. It's a wonder she doesn't give herself jaw ache. On second thoughts, I'll go when Irene isn't there."

As Peggy talked about what shifts Irene might be working, I felt my eyes starting to close. I put my cup down, opened my eyes wide and tried to focus on Peggy's words. My eyes had other ideas and began to close again. My eyelids felt like they were made of lead.

Peggy abruptly got to her feet and announced, "Off to bed you go, young lady. Where are those bloodstained clothes?"

"I've left them in a bag in the bathroom," I said. With some effort, I got to my feet.

"Sling the bag down the stairs, and I'll stick them in the washing machine for you."

"I can do that," I argued half-heartedly.

"I'm here. I'll do it. Just do as I say, Karis." Peggy put her hand on my arm and led me over to the stairs. "You don't have to be so independent all the time. If I was splattered in blood, wouldn't you take care of me? Yes, you would."

I thought Peggy was going to take me upstairs and tuck me into bed, but she didn't. She did watch me as I dragged myself upstairs. She was still there when I came to the top of the stairs with the bag of soiled clothes.

She held her arms out. "Chuck it down. I'll come back in a few hours and check on you."

I flung the bag at her and headed for my bed. I was asleep within minutes.

I woke up a few hours later and felt refreshed. A weird feeling ran through me. I sat up in bed and tried to pinpoint what it was.

Then it came to me.

It was time.

I got out of bed and went downstairs. I called out for Peggy in case she had returned, but she hadn't.

Good. It was better that I did this on my own.

I spotted the jumper which Peggy had knitted. I picked it up. It could be useful. I located the suitcase which I'd bought from the charity shop and took it over to the sofa. I sat down.

With the jumper on my lap and my hand on the suitcase, I closed my eyes.

The visions came to me one after the other in gruesome detail. Just as I'd had the last one, there was a knock at the door.

It was Seb. I took him into the kitchen and made us a drink. I definitely needed one after what I'd just seen.

I gave Seb his coffee and then sat opposite him. I said, "Has Martha confessed?"

"No, she hasn't. She said she doesn't know anything about Finley being murdered." He frowned. "I don't know why, but I believe her."

"Tell me everything she said."

"I began by asking her about the last time she'd seen Finley Booker alive. She last saw him one week before he went missing. She mentioned the dates she'd been on with him, mainly to the cinema, and said things were getting serious between them. She told me about the twin set she'd knitted, and admitted she'd lied to you and Peggy when you showed her the pattern."

"Did she say why she'd lied?"

"She panicked. It was the shock of seeing her pattern after all these years. It was the last item she'd ever made for herself. She couldn't bring herself to make anything after Finley went missing. Although, later on, she did knit jumpers for her husband, Leon." He gave me a smile. "She almost repeated the same words as you when she told me how she felt about Leon. The big love of her life was Finley, but when he disappeared, she started dating Leon. He'd known her for years and was constantly asking her out. When he proposed, she said yes even though she knew he was second-best. Over the years, she grew to love him."

I nodded. "The knitting patterns make sense now. She only knitted for her husband and daughter and not for herself. But she kept that twin set pattern. Part of her must have still been in love with Finley."

"You're right about that. Martha admitted it. When she answered the door to Morgan Booker earlier, she thought it was Finley. She let him into her house without a second thought. She soon knew she'd made a mistake when Morgan started asking her about his brother."

"Why did he turn up to her door like that after all these years?"

Seb gave me a wry smile. "Facebook. It's been a year since Leon died, and Martha's daughter posted lots of photos on her Facebook page in his memory. She put some information online about how Martha and Leon used to go to the cinema back in the day. She mentioned Martha's ex-boyfriend and said his name had been banned in their house by her dad. Morgan Booker had set up alerts for any mention of his brother's name. And, you can guess the rest. It didn't take Morgan long to find Martha. He'd been watching her house for a couple of days, and finally plucked up the courage to confront her early this morning." He picked his cup up and took a big drink.

As soon as he put it down, I said, "It was the leather jacket."

Seb gave me a look of surprise. "I was just about to tell you why Morgan thought it was Martha who killed Finley. Yes, it does have something to do with a leather jacket. What do you know about it?"

"I'll tell you that in a minute. You tell me what you know about the jacket."

"Okay. Finley had a distinctive leather jacket. It had been imported from the USA. It was Morgan who bought it for him as a birthday present. Finley first wore it on his date with Martha. It was on the night he went missing. Martha never saw the jacket."

"But Leon did. Was Leon wearing it in one of the photos his daughter put on Facebook?"

Seb gave me a nod.

"And that's what Morgan saw, isn't it? He knew that jacket belonged to Finley."

Seb gave me another nod. "How do you know that?"

I looked down at the table. "I've had a series of visions. From Leon's perspective." I looked back at Seb. "I felt his love for Martha. He'd loved her for years. He was riddled with jealousy when he saw how close she was getting to Finley. Martha confided in Leon and said she wanted to marry Finley. The rage I felt in Leon was—" I stopped and closed my eyes.

"You don't have to continue," Seb said softly.

I opened my eyes. "I have to. I saw Leon meeting Finley on the way to the cinema. Finley was wearing his new leather jacket. I saw —" I stopped again and gathered my courage. "I saw Leon kill Finley. I saw every horrific detail. Leon took Finley's jacket. He put Finley in a suitcase. He laughed as he did that." I inclined my head towards the living room. "The suitcase is in there. After seeing the murder, I got a snapshot of Leon's life with Martha. I could feel how satisfied he was when he saw genuine love in her eyes. He felt no remorse over what he'd done. Seb, after the investigation into Finley's disappearance died down, Leon wore that leather jacket with pride. He lied and said he'd bought it from America." Tears trickled down my cheeks.

Seb handed me a tissue. "That must have been awful for you to witness. I hate to ask this, but do you know where Finley's body is now?"

I wiped my tears away. "I know exactly where it is."

# Chapter 20

"Under the shed," I said. I looked at Erin, Robbie and Peggy's surprised faces. After going back to Martha's house with Seb and making the gruesome discovery, Seb had dropped me off at Erin's Café. We were sitting on the sofas in the quiet area.

"Under the shed?" Peggy repeated. "The shed in Martha's garden?"

I nodded. "It was in the bottom corner of the garden."

Erin asked, "How did you know it was there?"

"I saw Leon putting it there," I explained. "He didn't put the body there straight away because he didn't own the house when he murdered Finley." I swallowed and my throat felt too dry as the image of what Leon had done came back to me.

Robbie stood up. "You need a coffee. I'll make you one. I'll make us all one. I have defeated the coffee machine and it is now under my command." He gave me a kind smile before heading to the kitchen.

Erin was sitting at my side. She put her hand over mine and said, "You don't have to talk about it."

"I want to. I have to get it out. After Leon killed Finley, he put his body in that suitcase and took him into the woods. He took Finley's body out of the suitcase, wrapped him a blanket and buried him there. But when he bought the house with Martha, he decided to put Finley underneath the shed foundations."

Peggy shook her head in disbelief. "Why would he do that? Why didn't he leave Finley in the woods?"

"Maybe he was worried about Finley's body being discovered," I answered. I paused. "Actually, that's not the reason. When I was having my visions, I could feel Leon's emotions. He moved Finley's body out of pure spite. He wanted Finley to be near Martha and him as they started their married life together. He got a lot of satisfaction from knowing Finley was under that shed."

Erin muttered, "The evil so-and-so."

I continued, "I'm surprised the shed was still standing. Peggy, do you remember what Martha said about Leon being useless at DIY?"

Peggy nodded.

"When Seb and I went to the shed, it was leaning to one side. The foundations weren't level. A few more years and it would have collapsed on its own."

Peggy's eyes narrowed. "Perhaps Finley was trying to rise from the dead. What's going to happen now?"

I said, "Seb's going to get all the evidence together. I've given him the suitcase. He thinks there'll be evidence on it." My voice caught in my throat. "I can't stop thinking about what Leon did. I didn't know people could be so evil."

Erin put her arm around my shoulders and hugged me. "You poor thing. I don't know how you cope with these visions. I couldn't deal with them."

Robbie came over to us with a tray of drinks. He put them on the table.

Peggy looked at them and said, "Why are there five cups? Are you expecting company?"

"I am," Robbie replied. "And he's here now."

The café door opened and Seb came in. There was a grey tinge to his skin and he looked like he was carrying the weight of the world on his shoulders.

Robbie said to him, "You look like death warmed up. Come over here, take a seat and tell us what's happened. I've made you a coffee."

Seb sat next to Peggy and ran a hand over his forehead. He gave me a small smile and said, "How are you doing?"

I shrugged. "I'm okay. I wish I could wash Leon's memories away."

"They'll fade in time," Seb said. "Or you'll cope with them. You're strong enough to do that." He smiled at me again.

Peggy nudged him. "Stop flirting with Karis and tell us why you look so defeated."

Seb's shoulders sagged. "I've been talking to Martha. I had to explain to her what Leon had done." He looked down at his knees. "She was distraught, understandably so. Once the shock had worn off, she cried and cried. We had to get medical help for her. She's never going to be the same." He looked back up and I could see his eyes glistening.

In a soft voice, Peggy said, "It had to be done, lad. Someone had to tell her. I'm glad it was you. That poor woman." She shook her head. "To find out something like that must have broken her. Her whole marriage was a lie. Her devious husband slaughtered her one love and then heartlessly stuck him under the shed to rot away."

Robbie said, "There's no need to go into so much detail, Peggy. Seb, drink your coffee. How's Morgan Booker doing? Does he know about his brother yet?"

Seb picked his cup up and stared at it silently for a few seconds. He said, "No, he doesn't know. I'm going to the hospital soon to tell him. I'm not looking forward to that conversation."

Peggy patted him on the arm. "You'll manage. You've got the strength of character to do this. Have your coffee first."

Seb looked at Peggy. "Are you being nice to me? In front of everyone? Am I dreaming?"

Peggy chuckled. "Less of your cheek. I am capable of being nice, even to you. I'll tell you something else too. When you've finished at the station, you're invited to my house for dinner. I'll make you sausages with mashed potatoes and lots of gravy. Your mum said that's one of your favourite meals."

Seb's eyes grew wide. "It is. Are you being genuine? This isn't a cruel joke, is it? You shouldn't joke about sausages and mash."

"I'm not joking," Peggy retorted. "There's going to be dessert too. Karis, would you like to come over for dinner too? I don't want you being on your own tonight."

"I will. Thank you. I'm not sure how much I'll eat, but I'd love to be there."

A tiny twinkle came into Seb's eyes. He looked my way and said, "Give your leftovers to me. I'll take care of them."

Robbie looked into the distance and said dreamily, "Sausage and mash. With gravy."

Erin added in a matching tone, "And dessert too. Aren't Seb and Karis lucky?"

Peggy laughed. "Okay. You two lovebirds can come around too. I've got plenty."

"Are you sure it's not too much work for you?" I asked.

Peggy smiled. "It's no work at all. I love having company, and I love cooking for so many people. It'll be a bit of a squeeze in my house, but we'll manage."

Seb quickly drained his coffee and put his cup down. "Peggy, you've given me the boost I need to talk to Morgan Booker now. I will see you later at your house. I'll make sure I bring my appetite with me." He stood up. "Karis, can I have a word with you?"

"Of course." I followed him over to the café door and turned my back on the three pairs of eyes who were watching me.

Seb said quietly, "I can't imagine how horrific the images in your mind are, but I wanted to say thank you for all you've done. You saved Morgan Booker's life. And you found his brother. I know Martha's life is never going to be the same, but that's not your fault."

"I know." I sighed. "I can't stop my visions, but these last ones have been so difficult."

He put his hand on my arm. "You're not on your own with this. You've got me."

"And us!" Peggy called out. "Speak up, Seb. I can't hear everything you're saying."

Seb grinned at me and whispered, "I'll see you later." He waved at the group on the sofas before leaving the café.

When I returned to the sofas, I noticed an unusual silence. I looked at Erin and said, "What's going on now?"

"Nothing," Erin replied in a tone which confirmed something was going on.

Robbie said, "We were just saying how close you and Seb are getting."

"We're just friends," I said.

"Of course," Erin, Robbie and Peggy announced in one voice.

Peggy shuffled to the end of the sofa and said, "Let's talk about Karis' love life another time. And I don't want to talk about Martha anymore, it's too upsetting. I might call on her in a week or so and see how she's doing. Right, how are the plans for the café coming along? Are we going to open it next week?"

Robbie nodded. "We are."

"Great news," Peggy said. She looked at me. "Karis, try not to have any more murder visions before then. We don't have time for them." Her wrinkly face creased up in a smile.

I smiled back at her and said, "I'll try my best."